A1+

STUDENT'S BOOK

BEYOND

MACMILLAN

Robert Campbell
Rob Metcalf
Rebecca Robb Benne

AT THE PARTY

Grammar (2): *Be*: negative, questions and short answers; question words

Vocabulary (2): Numbers 21–100, days of the week, months phone contacts

LISTENING & VOCABULARY	GRAMMAR (2)	LANGUAGE & BEYOND	SPEAKING	WRITING
It's a small world! ***Listen to a description of where things are from*** **Vocabulary (2):** Countries and nationalities	*This/that, these/those* ***Talk about the things around you***	School skills: ***Be a good classmate***	Is it new? ***Describe things*** What's it like?	My things (description) ***Write a description of a thing***
Whose is it? ***Listen to a quiz show*** **Vocabulary (2):** Parts of the body	*Whose?*; possessive *'s/s'* and possessive pronouns ***Talk about your things, family and friends***	School skills: ***Be friendly to other students***	On the phone ***Talk on the phone*** You've got the wrong number	My favourite person (description) ***Write a description of a person***
A new neighbour ***Listen to a description of a room*** **Vocabulary (2):** Things in your room	*There is / there are* ***Describe a room***	School skills: ***Prepare your things for school***	You're welcome ***Ask for and give things*** Here you are	Don't forget (note) ***Write a note***
Are you musical? ***Listen to street interviews*** PRONOUNCE The /p/ sound **Vocabulary (2):** Music	Present simple ***Talk about habits and routines***	School skills: ***Make a clear note of your homework***	What time is it? ***Tell the time*** It's ten past seven	My free time (email) ***Write an email***
My daily routine ***Listen to a radio show*** **Vocabulary (2):** Daily activities	Adverbs of frequency ***Say how often you do things***	School skills: ***Ask for help***	Why not? ***Ask for and give reasons*** Because ...	A normal day (message) ***Write a website post***

LISTENING & VOCABULARY	GRAMMAR (2)	LANGUAGE & BEYOND	SPEAKING	WRITING
Favourite food ***Understand a conversation about food*** **Vocabulary (2):** Food and drink	*Some* and *any*, *much* and *many* ***Talk about how much there is of something*** PRONOUNCE The /ʌ/ sound	School skills: ***Try new things***	How much is it? ***Ask how much something is*** Sorry, that's too much.	Back home (text message) ***Write a text message***
Mime show ***Listen to descriptions*** **Vocabulary (2):** Action verbs	Present continuous ***Ask and answer questions about things happening now***	School skills: ***Be polite***	I love acting ***Talk about things you like*** Do you like it?	A day in the city (message) ***Write a short message***
A great day out ***Listen to a description of a day out*** **Vocabulary (2):** The country	Past simple ***Talk about events in the past*** PRONOUNCE Past simple verbs	School skills: ***Be careful with money***	How are things? ***Ask how people are*** I'm fine thanks	Send me a postcard (postcard) ***Write a postcard***
What did they say? ***Understand short conversations*** **Vocabulary (2):** Adjectives of opinion PRONOUNCE The long /eɪ/ sound	Past simple ***Ask about things in the past***	School skills: ***Act in an honest way***	Yes, please ***Offer something to somebody*** What would you like?	My weekend (chat message) ***Write chat messages about your weekend***
Sports camp ***Listen to a talk*** **Vocabulary (2):** Sports	*Be going to* ***Talk about plans for the future***	School skills: ***Do your best when things are hard***	Where is it? ***Ask for and give directions*** It's on the left	Latest update (blog post) ***Write a blog post***

S STARTER GET READY: IT'S MY PARTY

HELLO!

THINK AND READ

1 1.01 **Read the story. What's Emily's favourite colour?**

2 **Read the story again. Do the exercises when you see this icon ★.**

RECALL

1 ★ NUMBERS 1–20

a 1.02 **Work in pairs. Complete the numbers with *a*, *e*, *i*, *o* and *u*. Then listen and repeat.**

1 _o_ n _e_	6 s ___ x	11 ___ l ___ v ___ n	16 s ___ xt ___ ___ n
2 tw ___	7 s ___ v ___ n	12 tw ___ lv ___	17 s ___ v ___ nt ___ ___ n
3 thr ___ ___	8 ___ ___ ght	13 th ___ rt ___ ___ n	18 ___ ___ ght ___ ___ n
4 f ___ ___ r	9 n ___ n ___	14 f ___ ___ rt ___ ___ n	19 n ___ n ___ t ___ ___ n
5 f ___ v ___	10 t ___ n	15 f ___ ft ___ ___ n	20 tw ___ nty

b **Work in pairs. Student A: say a number from 1 to 20. Student B: close your book. Write the number in letters. Student A: check the number. Then swap roles.**

2 ★ INTRODUCTIONS

a **Put the words in order to make sentences.**

Maria: Hi. *Maria. / I'm*
Hi. (1) *I'm Maria.*
Eric: Hello. *Eric. / My / name's*
Hello. (2) ___
Maria: *is / This / Mark.*
(3) ___

b 1.03 **Listen and check. Then listen and repeat.**

3 ★ *I/MY, YOU/YOUR*

Complete the table. Use words from pictures 1, 4 and 5.

	I'm Leo.	This is my sister.
Singular	*I*	*my*
	you	___
	___	his
	she	her
	___	its
Plural	we	___
	you	your
	they	their

4 1.04 **Complete Chloe's sentences with words from the table in Exercise 3. Then listen and check your answers.**

1 'Lucy's here with *her* friend, Maria.'
2 'This is Mark, and this is ________ brother.'
3 'The pizzas? ________ 're on the table.'
4 'Hi Eric. ________ sunglasses are great!'
5 'The cat? It lives next door. ________ name's Star.'

5 ★ **COLOURS**

1.05 **Match the colours to the words in the box. Listen and repeat.**

black ___	blue ___	brown ___	green ___	orange ___
pink ___	purple ___	red ___	white ___	yellow ___

6 ★ ***BE***

a Complete the sentences with *'m/am*, *'re/are* or *'s/is*.

Chloe: They (1) *'re* my friends from school. We (2) ________ in the same class.
Ben: Eric (3) ________ number 7 in the team, and I (4) ________ number 11.
Chloe: His name (5) ________ Mark. You (6) ________ at the same school.
Ben: Kayla (7) ________ from Canada. Chloe and Kayla (8) ________ really good friends.

b 1.06 **Listen and check.**

7 ★ **HAVE A PARTY**

Write an invitation for your party. Use the invitation in the story to help you.

Workbook, pages 4–5

See GRAMMAR DATABASE, page 120.

AT THE PARTY

THINK AND READ

1 1.07 **Read the story. Who's Maximus?**

2 **Read the story again. Do the exercises when you see this icon ★.**

RECALL

1 ★ **NUMBERS 21–100**

1.08 **Match the numbers to the words. Then listen and repeat.**

20 30 40 50 60 70 80 90 100

thirty twenty forty one hundred sixty seventy fifty ninety eighty

2 ★ **DAYS OF THE WEEK**

a 1.09 **Write the days of the week in order. Listen and check. Then listen and repeat.**

Friday	Saturday	Sunday
Thursday	Wednesday	

Monday ....
Tuesday ....
....
....

b **Work in pairs. Close your books. Write the days. Then check your spelling.**

3 ★ **MONTHS**

a **Work in pairs. Write the months in order.**

April	August	December	~~February~~	March	May
~~January~~	July	June	October	September	November

January, February, ...

b 1.10 **Listen and check. Then listen and repeat.**

4 ★ ***BE:* NEGATIVE, QUESTIONS AND SHORT ANSWERS**

1.11 **Complete the conversation. Then listen and check.**

am are aren't ~~is~~ isn't 'm not

Leo: Hi. I'm Maximus.
Emily: (1) *Is* that your real name?
Leo: No, it (2) .... And I (3) .... really a gladiator.
Emily: (4) .... you one of Ben's friends?
Leo: Yes, I (5) .... , but we (6) .... friends from school.

5 QUESTION WORDS

a Match the question words (1–5) to the pictures (a–e).

1 Who? *e*
2 What? ……
3 Where? ……
4 When? ……
5 How old? ……

b 1.12 **Complete the conversation with question words. Then listen and check.**

Emily: (1) *How old* are you?
Leo: I'm 13.
Emily: (2) ………… 's your birthday?
Leo: It's in October. And your birthday's in May.
Emily: That's right! (3) ………… are you?
Leo: I'm Maximus.
Emily: (4) ………… 's your *real* name?

6 PHONE CONTACTS

Work in pairs. Complete the contact information for your partner.

What's your … ?

How old … ?

When's your … ?

Name: …………
Phone number: …………
Age: …………
Birthday: …………
Address: …………

Workbook, pages 6–7

See GRAMMAR DATABASE, page 120.

UNIT 1

AN A–Z OF ME

IN THE PICTURE My things

Talk about your things

WORK WITH WORDS Categories

1 a RECALL **Work in pairs. Write the name of the things in the photos. The words start with the letter (A–Z) on each photo. You have three minutes.**

A – address …

b 1.13 **Listen and check your answers.**

c Work in pairs. Ask and answer questions about the photos.

What's this in English?

It's a key / an orange.

They're jeans.

2 a Work in pairs. Write the words in Exercise 1a in the best categories.

Animals	Clothes	Food
Games	**Home**	**People**
	address	
School	**Technology**	**Transport**

b Compare your answers with the rest of the class.

c 1.14 **Listen and repeat the categories.**

3 a Work in groups. Add other words to the categories.

b Make a class list. Which group has the most words for each category?

4 THE MOVING PICTURE **Watch the video. Write the categories in the correct order.**

5 a 1.15 PRONOUNCE **Listen to the alphabet rap. Repeat the letters.**

b Work in pairs.
Student A: spell a word from this lesson.
Student B: write it. Say 'stop' when you know it.

B – I – K …

Stop! Is it 'bike'?

Yes, that's right. / No. Try again!

PHRASE BYTES

What's your favourite word for animals/clothes?

My word's …

What's your word?

How do you say … in English?

WRITE AND SPEAK

6 **Work in pairs. Write your favourite word for each category in Exercise 2a. Then compare with your partner.**

GO BEYOND

Do the Words & Beyond exercise on page 130.

Workbook, page 8

READING World Wide Words

>>> Read an article from a book

SPEAK AND READ

1 Work in pairs. Look at the words in the box. Then answer the questions.

bus café coffee hotel music radio taxi train

1 What are the words in your language?
2 Which words are the same or very similar in your language? Circle them.

PHRASE BYTES

What's *bus* in our language?
It's … / I don't know.
Café is the same / very similar in …
Train is different in …

2 1.16 Read the start of the article. What's an international word?

WORLD WIDE WORDS FOR KIDS

International words **are the same or very similar in many different languages. With international words you can talk to people from different countries. Use these international words on holiday or with tourists in your city.**

1 Take a ***taxi*** or ***metro***. (***Bus*** and ***train*** are similar in some languages, but they aren't international words.)

2 Find a ***wi-fi*** hotspot. Use the ***internet*** on your ***telephone*** to check ***emails***, listen to the ***radio*** or watch ***music videos***.

3 Go to a ***café*** or a ***bar***. Drink ***tea*** or ***coffee***.

4 Go to a ***restaurant***. Eat a ***pizza*** with a ***salad***.

5 Visit a ***museum***, go to a ***park*** or watch a ***film*** at the ***cinema***. Or stay in your ***hotel*** and watch a ***football*** match on ***television***!

3 Read the rest of the article. Match sections 1–5 to the categories in the box.

__ Drinks __ Food __ Places __ Technology __ Transport

4 Read the article again. Which words in Exercise 1 are international words?

REACT

5 Work in pairs. Choose your five favourite international words. Then compare with your partner.

GO BEYOND

Read the article again. Make a phrasebook of international words.
Transport: *taxi, metro*
Technology: *…*

Workbook, page 9

GRAMMAR Plural nouns; *a/an, the*

>>> Talk about one or more things

READ >>> Grammar in context

1 Read Stella's list of likes and dislikes. Which of your likes and dislikes are the same?

SOCIAL SCENE

LIKES

- maths classes (We've got a great teacher.)
- the people in my drama group
- an ice cream on a hot day
- old jeans
- the internet

DISLIKES

- big cities (They're really noisy!)
- the school bus (It's always full.)
- video games (boring! ☹)
- sunglasses
- school lunches

STUDY

2 Complete the table with nouns from Exercise 1.

Plural nouns	
game > …………	
box > *boxes* / ………… > *buses*	class > ………… / lunch > …………
key > *keys*	city > …………
man > *men* / woman > *women*	person > ………… / jeans > …………

See GRAMMAR DATABASE, page 120.

3 Complete with words from Exercise 1.

a/an, the

*We've got **a** great maths teacher.*
*I like **an** ………… on a hot day.*
***The** ………… bus is always full.*
*I like **the** people in my ………… .*
*~~**The**~~ Old ………… are my favourite clothes.*
*I don't like ~~**the**~~ ………… games.*

See GRAMMAR DATABASE, page 120.

PRACTISE

4 Write the singular nouns.

	singular	plural
1	*category*	categories
2	…………	videos
3	…………	matches
4	…………	phones
5	…………	Xboxes
6	…………	women

5 Write the things in the photos.

apple ~~day~~ glass man sandwich story

1 *three days*

2 …………

3 …………

4 …………

5 …………

6 …………

6 Choose the correct options in the profile.

PROFILE

I'm from Washington. It's (1) *a* / *the* capital city of the USA. It's (2) *a* / *the* very big city. I love (3) *the* / *–* dinosaurs and I've got (4) *a* / *the* big poster of a T-rex in my room. I like (5) *the* / *–* video games too. I've got (6) *a* / *an* Xbox and (7) *a* / *an* PlayStation. My favourite sport is basketball. I play for (8) *a* / *the* school basketball team.

7 Complete the sentences with *a/an, the* or –.

ALL ABOUT ME!

1 I like – apples.
2 I don't like ………… colour orange.
3 I take ………… taxi to school.
4 I love ………… internet.
5 I've got ………… old phone.
6 I don't like ………… pizzas.

WRITE AND SPEAK

8 a Write five sentences about you, three true and two false.

I'm … *I've got …*
My favourite … *I like / don't like …*

b Work in pairs. Say your sentences. Your partner says 'true' or 'false'.

>>> Workbook, pages 10–11

>>> Listen to a description of where things are from

WORK WITH WORDS Countries and nationalities

1 a ▶1.17 **Work in pairs. Write the correct numbers in the table. Then listen and check.**

Number	Country	Nationality
	Brazil	Brazilian
	Germany	Germ.........
	Italy	Ital.........
	Japan	Japan.........
	South Africa	South Africa.........
	Turkey	Turk.........

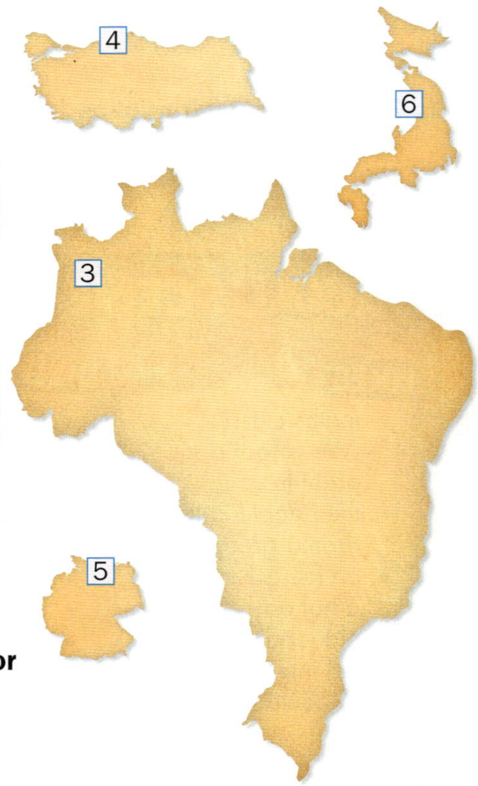

b ▶1.18 **Try and complete the nationalities. Add *-an*, *-ese*, *-ian*, *-n* or *-ish* to the words. Listen and check. Then listen and repeat.**

2 Work in pairs. Think of something famous for each country. Then make a class list.

LISTENING TIP

Before you listen, think: 'What do I know about this topic?' Use your answer to help you understand.

SPEAK AND LISTEN

3 a Work in pairs. Guess where Stefan's things are from. Use countries from Exercise 1.

b ▶1.19 **Stefan is talking about where his things are from. Listen and check your ideas.**

4 ▶1.19 **Listen again and choose the correct answer.**

1 Stefan's from …
   (A) the UK. **B** Italy. **C** Turkey.
2 Stefan says 'It's a small world' because his things are all from …
   A the same part of the world.
   B different parts of the world.
   C very far away.
3 Where's Stefan's friend Ron?
   A in London **B** in Tokyo **C** in New York

PHRASE BYTES

My jeans/sunglasses are from …
Where's your T-shirt/bag from?
What's on the label?
It says … on the label.
I don't know.

REACT

5 Work in pairs. Say where your things are from.

GO BEYOND

Do the Words & Beyond exercise on page 130.

Workbook, pages 12–13

GRAMMAR *This/that, these/those*

Talk about the things around you

READ AND LISTEN Grammar in context

1 1.20 **Read and listen to the conversation. Write the names of the fruit.**

Zoe: We need to buy fruit for lunch.
Anya: OK. What about those bananas?
Zoe: I don't like bananas. But these apples are nice.
Anya: They're very green. What's the name of those red things?
Zoe: Those are grapes. They aren't my favourite fruit.
Anya: And what's this?
Zoe: It's a watermelon. But look at that fruit salad. That's got lots of different fruit in it.
Anya: Yes. Let's buy fruit salad.

STUDY

2 Complete the table with words from Exercise 1.

This/that, these/those

Here	There

Singular	Singular
What's ***this****?*	*Look at* ***that*** ....
Plural	Plural
These apples *are nice.*	***Those*** *are* ....

See GRAMMAR DATABASE, page 120.

PRACTISE

3 Complete the sentences with *this*, *that*, *these* and *those*.

1 I like those T-shirts.
2 .... blue T-shirt's nice.
3 What about .... sunglasses?
4 I don't like .... bag.
5 .... jeans are cool.
6 Do you like .... football shirt?

4 Complete the conversation with *this*, *that*, *these* and *those*.

Zoe: Wow! Look at this stall.
Anya: Yes! I love (1) those . What are they called?
Zoe: Postcards. And (2) ....'s a really old tennis racket!
Anya: What's (3) .... in English?
Zoe: It's a bowl.
Anya: It's nice. And what are (4) .... ?
Zoe: They're sports cards. And (5) .... is an album for the cards.

SPEAK

5 Work in pairs. Put your things on your desk. Ask and answer questions about them.

What's this?
It's my ...
What are those?
They're my ...
What's that?

Workbook, page 14

Be a good classmate

SPEAK AND READ

1 a Work in pairs. Match the situations (1–5) in the picture to the descriptions (a–f).

b Do you do these things in class? Write *never* (0%), *sometimes* (50%) or *always* (100%). Then compare your answers with the rest of your class.

a be noisy ....
b help classmates ....
c listen to the teacher ....
d throw rubbish in the bin ....
e use a phone ....
f be quiet ....

DO

2 a Work in pairs. Write the things in Exercise 1a in the correct column. Can you add more things?

It's good to … in class.	It's bad to … in class.

b Why are the things good or bad? Complete the sentences. Use your own words or the words in the box.

1 You can/can't …
2 The teacher can/can't …
3 Other students can/can't …
4 The classroom is/isn't …

hear other students
hear the teacher clean and tidy
understand the lesson

PHRASE BYTES

I'm / I'm not …
It's important because …
We need to … more.

REFLECT

3 Talk about the questions. Then read the REFLECTION POINT.

1 Are you a good classmate?
2 Why is it important to be a good classmate?
3 What can you change in your class?

EXTEND

4 Work in groups. Choose a situation: with your friends or at home. Write two good things and two bad things for your situation.

It's good/bad to …

REFLECTION POINT

If you're a good classmate, you respect the teacher and other students. When you're a good classmate, all the students in the class can learn.

SCHOOL SKILLS

Workbook page 17

SPEAKING Is it new?

Describe things

SPEAK

1 Work in pairs. Match the adjectives to their opposites.

1 big a new
2 old b horrible
3 quiet c small
4 nice d noisy

WATCH OR LISTEN

2 1.21 Watch or listen to the scenes. What things do the people describe?

1
Becca: I can't find my … .
Kent: What colour is it?
Becca: It's black and it's really (1) ______ .
Kent: Is that it on the chair?
Becca: Yes, that's it.

2
Jiya: Do you like Zac's … ? They're (2) ______ .
Becca: I know. They're Italian. They're very (3) ______ .
Jiya: I think they're (4) ______ .

3
Zac: What's your … like?
Jiya: It's OK, but the neighbours are really (5) ______ .
Zac: What about your room? Is it (6) ______ ?
Jiya: No, my room's very (7) ______ .

3 1.21 Complete the conversations with the adjectives in Exercise 1. Then watch or listen again and check.

4 1.22 Listen and repeat the sentences from the conversations.

ACT

5 Work in pairs. Complete the tasks.

- Choose a conversation from Exercise 2.
- Write a similar conversation about a different thing.
- Practise the conversation.
- Present the conversation to other students. Don't read it.

PHRASEBOOK 1.23

Ask for a description of something
What colour is it?
What's / What are your … like?
Is it big/small … ?

Describe something
It's black/red …
They're Italian/German …
They're very/really nice.
The neighbours are noisy/quiet …

Workbook, page 15

WRITING My things

>>> Write a description of a thing

SPEAK AND READ

1 a **Work in pairs. Look at the photos and describe them. Note the adjectives (*big*, *blue*, etc) you use.**

b **Read the descriptions. Do they use the same adjectives?**

This is my new bike. It's a mountain bike and it's cool and *really* fast.

This is a great photo of Nele and Leni, the African elephants in my local zoo. Nele's the big one.

This is my favourite T-shirt. That's my name in Japanese on the front (Sara).

2 **Read the tips in the HOW TO box. Then underline other adjectives in the photo descriptions.**

HOW TO

write a description of a thing

- Use *am/are/is* + adjective: *it's* ***cool***.
- Use adjective + noun: *my* ***favourite T-shirt***.
- Use *really/very* + adjective: ***really fast***.

PRACTISE

3 **Put the words in order to make sentences.**

1 phone. / my / is / This / new

2 nice / are / sunglasses. / really / These

3 of Japanese / This / collection / my / comics. / is

4 very / My / fast. / isn't / computer

5 really / jeans / are / favourite / old. / My

Get it right

Adjectives don't change.

two elephants *two African~~s~~ elephants*

PLAN

4 **You're going to write descriptions for some pictures. Use the *Writing plan* to help you prepare.**

WRITING PLAN

1 **Choose three pictures.**
Use photos of your things, or draw pictures of them. ☐

2 **Describe the things.**
What colour are they? Are they old/new/big/small? ☐

3 **Use adjectives correctly.**
Read the tips in the HOW TO box. ☐

WRITE AND CHECK

5 **Write your descriptions. Then check them. Tick (✓) the things in the plan.**

SHARE

6 **Swap your descriptions with other students. Choose your favourite picture and description.**

Workbook, page 16–17

VOCABULARY Categories

1 Complete the categories.

YourThings THE WEBSITE FOR YOU AND YOUR THINGS

HOME
ABOUT
PROFILE
SEARCH
YOUR THINGS

1 
a __ __ __ __ __ __ __ __

2 
h __ __ __

3 
c __ __ __ __ __ __ __

4 
p __ __ __ __ __ __

5 
f __ __ __ __

6 
t __ __ __ __ __ __ __ __ __

7 
g __ __ __ __ __

8 
t __ __ __ __ __ __ __ __

___ /8

Countries and nationalities

2 Complete the countries and nationalities.

1 Juliana's my Braz______ pen friend. She's from Rio de Janeiro in Braz______ .
2 These jeans are from Ital______ . I love Ital______ fashion.
3 My dad's South Afric______ , and South Afric______ is my favourite football team.
4 I want to go to Turk______ . I love Turk______ food!
5 I'm Yoshi and I'm Jap______ . I'm from Osaka in the south of Jap______ .
6 Are you from Germ______ ? I want to practise my Germ______ .

___ /12

GRAMMAR Plural nouns; *a/an, the*

3 Complete the message with *a*, *an*, *the*, – or the plural of the noun in brackets ().

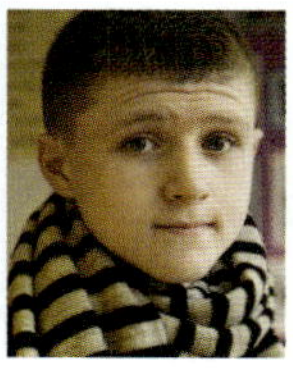

My name's Vasily and I live in (1) ______ city in Russia called Gatchina. It isn't one of Russia's famous (2) ______ (city), but it's (3) ______ interesting place. I love technology and (4) ______ computers. (5) ______ science teachers at my school are great and I learn a lot in their (6) ______ (class). I love (7) ______ internet too. I've got (8) ______ website with lots of my (9) ______ (video) on it.

___ /18

This/that, these/those

4 Complete the description with *this*, *that*, *these* and *those*.

YourThings

'Hi everyone! (1) ______ is my room. All my favourite things are in here. (2) ______ are my favourite jeans. I love them! (3) ______ phone isn't very new, but I still use it. (4) ______ sunglasses are from my local market. They're really cool. (5) ______'s my games console. And you see (6) ______ football? It's got Neymar's signature on it. ☺'

___ /12

Your score: ___ /50

SKILLS CHECK

✓✓✓ Yes, I can. No problem!
✓✓ Yes, I can. But I need a bit of help.
✓ Yes, I can. But I need a lot of help.

I can read an article from a book. ______
I can listen to a description of where things are from. ______
I can be a good classmate. ______
I can describe things. ______
I can write a description of a thing. ______

Workbook, pages 18–19

UNIT 2 PEOPLE

IN THE PICTURE Family and friends

Talk about your family and friends

WORK WITH WORDS Family

1 RECALL **Work in pairs. Write the opposites. You have one minute.**

1 same – ....
2 nice – ....
3 .... – small
4 bad – ....
5 .... – quiet
6 old – .... (for things)

Get it right

For people, the opposite of *old* is *young*.

2 a **Work in pairs. Look at the photos on Leon's phone. Which are friends? Which are family members?**

b 1.24 **Listen and check your answers. Match the names to the correct photos.**

Asha .... Felix .... Nico ....

PHRASE BYTES

I think the boy/girl in photo 1 … is a friend/family member.

I think the man/woman in photo … is …

3 a 1.24 **Listen again. Match the family words to the photos.**

brother .... dad .... father .... grandchild ....
grandad .... grandfather .... grandma .... grandmother ....
mother .... mum .... only child .... sister ....

b 1.25 **Listen and check.**

4 a 1.26 PRONOUNCE **Listen and repeat the long /ɑː/ sound in these words.**

father grandfather grandma

b 1.27 **Listen and repeat these words.**

are banana car drama park postcard

5 **Work in pairs. Ask and answer.**

Who's in photo 3?

That's Leon's grandma and grandad.

6 THE MOVING PICTURE **Watch the video about Leon's friend Felix. Who are the other people? Are they friends or family?**

SPEAK

7 **Work in pairs. Draw a picture of your family or show photos. Talk about your family.**

PHRASE BYTES

This is my dad/sister …

He's/She's … years old.

He's/She's from Chile …

He's/She's quiet/noisy/great/horrible/small / very nice …

GO BEYOND

Do the Words & Beyond exercise on page 131.

Workbook, page 20

READING I've got a new phone

Read text messages

SPEAK AND READ

1 Work in pairs. Write eight names for your phone contact list. Then tell your partner about your list.

2 1.28 Look at the photos and read the first sentence of each message. Who are the messages from? Who are they for?

PHRASE BYTES

Lucy is a friend from football …

Alex is my brother …

Ravi is from Number 3 in my street.

READING TIP

Look at the type of text. It can help you understand what it's about.

3 **Read the messages and write the name(s).**

1 .... are game players.
2 .... isn't Nico.
3 .... is in his room.
4 .... is at a birthday party.
5 .... have got lots of homework.
6 .... isn't happy about text messages in class.

4 **Write the words from the messages in Exercise 2.**

1 *camera*
2 ph..........
3 g.......... s
4 in..........
5 t.......... m.......... s

PHRASE BYTES

In my school it's OK / it isn't OK to use phones in …

I use my phone for calls/photos …

REACT

5 Work in pairs. Ask and answer the questions.

1 Is it OK to use phones at your school? When and where?
2 What do you or your friends use your phones for?

GO BEYOND

Write a message from Leon to a different person from pages 20–21. Write one or two sentences.

Workbook, page 21

GRAMMAR *Have got*

>>> Talk about your things, ideas and problems

READ AND LISTEN >>> Grammar in context

1 1.29 **Read and listen to the conversation. Complete the sentences.**

It's Clara's dad's .... on Saturday. Clara hasn't got a ....

Clara: I've got a problem.
Aazim: What?
Clara: I haven't got a present for my dad's birthday on Saturday.
Aazim: Has he got a pen for his tablet? That's a good present.
Clara: No, he hasn't. He hasn't got a tablet. He's got a laptop.
Aazim: OK. Have you got an idea?
Clara: No, I haven't. And I haven't got much time for shopping.
Aazim: Oh. You're right. You've got a problem.

STUDY

2 Complete the tables with examples from Exercise 1.

Get it right

*Clara's got a problem. = Clara **has got** a problem.*

*Clara and Aazim **have got** a problem.*

Have got **(I, you, we, they)**	
✓ Positive	✗ Negative
I 've got a problem.	*I .... a present.*
? Questions	Short answers
.... you .... an idea?	*Yes, I have.* *No, I ....*

Have got **(he, she, it)**	
✓ Positive	✗ Negative
He .... a laptop.	*He .... a tablet.*
? Questions	Short answers
.... he got a pen?	*Yes, he has.* *No, he ....*

See GRAMMAR DATABASE, page 121.

PRACTISE

3 Complete Clara's sentences with *'ve got / have got* or *haven't got*.

I (1) *'ve got* a great room! It's very big, but I (2) .... a TV. We (3) .... one television in our house – but it isn't in my room! I (4) .... a computer. It's old. My brothers (5) .... an Xbox. It's new and they (6) .... a lot of games – only four or five.

4 Write about Aazim. What has he got? What hasn't he got?

He's got three sisters.

1  ✓

2 

3  ✓

4 

5 

6  ✓

5 1.30 **Complete the conversation. Then listen and check.**

Clara: (1) *Have* you got a favourite film?
Lila: Erm, no, I (2) .... What about you?
Clara: Yes, I (3) .... It's *School Days*.
Lila: (4) .... it got Kristin Stone in it?
Clara: No, it (5) .... It's with Mila King.
Lila: Oh, yes. (6) .... you got it?
Clara: Yes, I (7) .... We can watch it together.

6 Write three more questions for a partner.

Survey

- *Have you got a TV in your room?*
- *Have you got a big family?*
- *Have you got a favourite film?*

SPEAK

7 Work in pairs. Ask and answer the questions you both wrote in Exercise 6.

>>> Workbook, pages 22–23

LISTENING AND VOCABULARY Whose is it?

Listen to a quiz show

WORK WITH WORDS Parts of the body

1 **Look at Mina's pictures of parts of the body. What do you think?**

PHRASE BYTES

I think they're good/clever …

I like / don't like them.

2 a 1.31 **Listen and point to the correct body parts in the pictures.**

b 1.32 **Listen and repeat the parts of the body.**

arm back ear eye face foot hand
head leg mouth nose teeth

3 a **Work in pairs. Student A: look at page 141. Read the description to your partner. Student B: draw and colour the picture.**

b **Student B: look at page 142. Read the description to your partner. Student A: draw and colour the picture.**

SPEAK AND LISTEN

4 **Work in pairs. Look at the photos and choose the correct answer.**

Get it right

one tooth – two teeth

one foot – two feet

FAMOUS BODY PARTS QUIZ

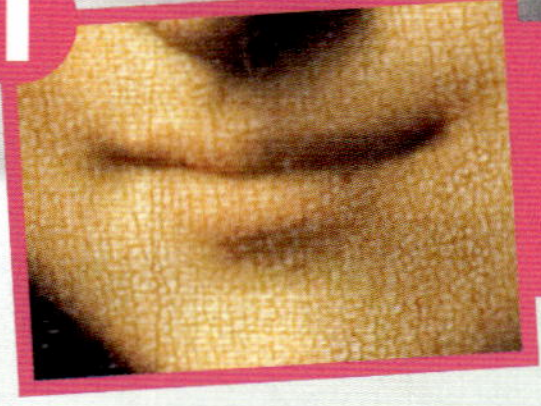

1 Whose mouth is this?
A Beyoncé's
B the Mona Lisa's
C Angelina Jolie's

2 Whose hands are these?
A Batman's
B Mario's
C Mickey Mouse's

3 Whose legs are these?
A Mario Balotelli's
B Neymar da Silva Santos Júniors's
C Lionel Messi's

4 Whose ear is this?
A Frodo Baggins' (*The Hobbit*)
B Mr Spock's (*Star Trek*)
C Daniel Craig's (*James Bond*)

5 Whose eye is this?
A Jennifer Lawrence's
B Cleopatra's
C Lady Gaga's

5 1.33 **Listen to the quiz. Check your answers. Who's the winner – Hazel or Rufus?**

6 1.33 **Listen again. What's special about the things in the photos?**

1 *Her smile is special.*   2 *His hands are …*

PHRASE BYTES

I think / don't think it's a good game.

I've got blue eyes / nice feet.

I've got big feet. My dad's got big feet too.

I've got long legs like my mum.

REACT

7 **Work in pairs. Ask and answer the questions.**

1 Is this a good quiz game?
2 What's special about your eyes, ears, feet, etc?
3 Have you got the same eyes, legs, etc as people in your family?

GO BEYOND

Do the Words & Beyond exercise on page 131.

Workbook, pages 24–25

GRAMMAR *Whose?*; possessive *'s/s'* and possessive pronouns

»» Talk about your things, family and friends

READ AND LISTEN »» Grammar in context

1 1.34 **Read and listen to the conversation. Which legs in the photo are Amy's legs?**

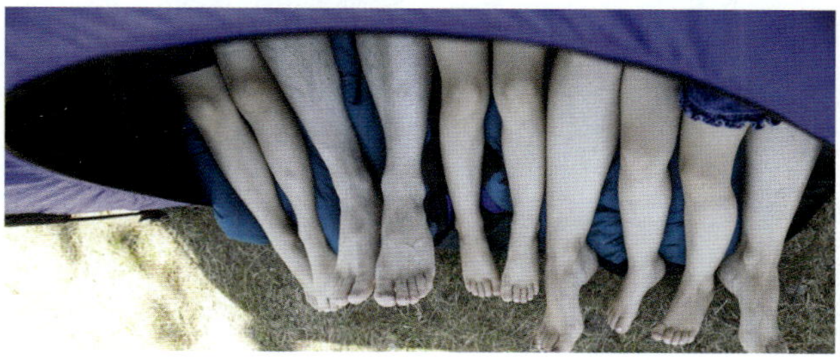

Amy: Hi Nita! This is a photo from our camping holiday!
Nita: Cool! Whose legs are they?
Amy: My mum's, my dad's, my sister's, her friend's – and mine. My two brothers' legs aren't in the photo.
Nita: Which legs are yours?
Amy: My sister's friend Ella is in the middle. On the right are my mum's and my sister's legs – theirs are together. Dad is on the other side of Ella – those legs with the big feet are his. And mine are the nice legs!

STUDY

2 Complete the table with examples from Exercise 1.

Whose? and possessive *'s/s'*
***Whose* + noun + question** Whose *legs are they?*
noun + 's I've got one sister → *My* .... *legs …*
regular plural noun + s' I've got two brothers → *My* .... *legs …*

See GRAMMAR DATABASE, page 121.

3 Complete the table with pronouns from Exercise 1.

Possessive pronouns

My legs are the nice legs. → ***Mine** are the nice legs.*

Possessive adjectives	Possessive pronouns
my	....
your	....
his/her	.... / hers
our	ours
their	....

See GRAMMAR DATABASE, page 121.

PRACTISE

4 Complete Amy's sentences with *'s* or *s'* and a part of the body.

1 That's my sister's tooth (my sister).

2 Those are .... (my grandad).

3 Those are .... (my brothers).

4 Those are .... (my friends).

5 Those are .... (my grandparents).

6 That's .... (my mum).

5 Complete the answers with the correct possessive pronouns.

Teacher: Whose homework is this?
Student: I think it's Lucy's homework. Yes, it's (1) hers .
Teacher: Whose pen is this?
Student: I think it's my pen. Yes, it's (2) ....
Teacher: Whose bags are these?
Student: I think they're Diego's and Felipe's. Yes, they're (3) ....
Teacher: Whose tablet is this?
Student: I think it's Mr Chan's. Yes, it's (4) ....
Teacher: Whose books are these?
Student: I think they're our books. Yes, they're (5) ....
Teacher: Whose glasses are these?
Student: I think they're your glasses. Yes, they're (6) .... , Miss!

SPEAK

6 Play *Whose chair is it?*

- Look where other students are in the class.
- Walk around. When your teacher says 'STOP', sit down. Say whose chair you're in.

I'm in Valentina's chair.

Yes, that's hers.

That isn't hers. That's Galina's chair.

»» Workbook, page 26

LANGUAGE & BEYOND

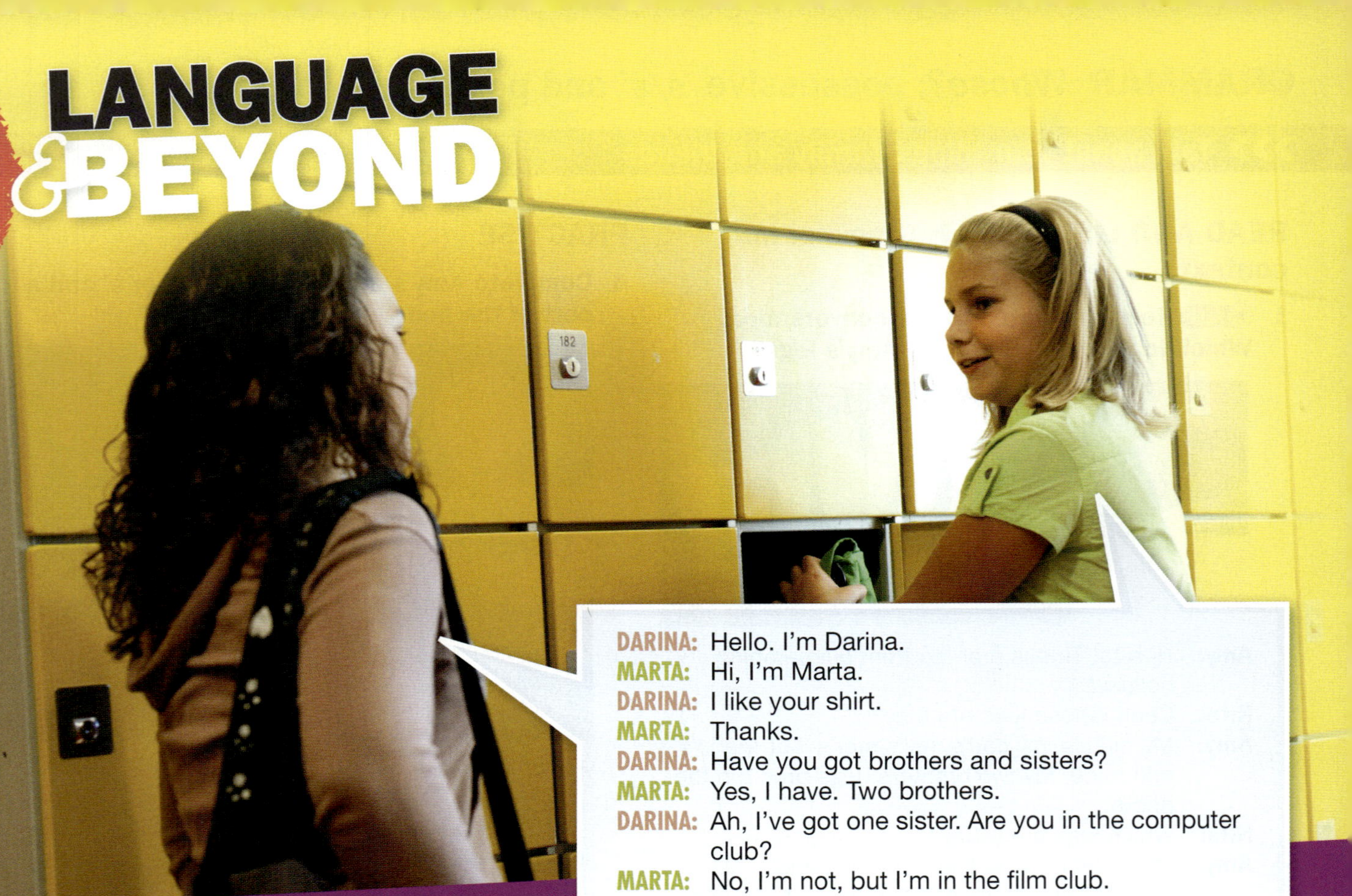

DARINA: Hello. I'm Darina.
MARTA: Hi, I'm Marta.
DARINA: I like your shirt.
MARTA: Thanks.
DARINA: Have you got brothers and sisters?
MARTA: Yes, I have. Two brothers.
DARINA: Ah, I've got one sister. Are you in the computer club?
MARTA: No, I'm not, but I'm in the film club.
DARINA: OK. What's your favourite film?
MARTA: *High School Story.*
DARINA: That's mine too! … What's your phone number?
MARTA: It's 334752.

››› Be friendly to other students

READ

1 (1.35) **Read and listen to the conversation. What have the girls got in common?**

DO

2 Put the 'Make friends' tips in the correct order. (Use Exercise 1 to help you.)

3 Match the sentences to tips a–e in Exercise 2.

1. Your shoes are nice. ___
2. What's your favourite TV show? ___
3. What's your address? ___
4. Hello. ___
5. Who's your favourite football player? ___
6. Are you in the football team? ___

MAKE FRIENDS – IT'S EASY!

___ a Ask for an address or phone number.
___ b Ask questions about favourite films or stars, or clubs and teams.
___ c Say something nice.
___ d Smile ☺ and say hello.
___ e Ask questions about family.

REFLECT

4 Talk about the questions. Then read the REFLECTION POINT.

1. Have you got lots of friends? Or have you got one or two good friends?
2. Where are your friends from (school, clubs, teams, your street)?
3. Is it easy or hard for you to make new friends?

PHRASE BYTES

I've got …
My friends are from school …
It's easy for me to make new friends. I like to talk to people.
It's hard for me. I'm quiet.

EXTEND

5 a Make notes in English about your family and your favourite things: films, TV programmes, stars, sports teams, etc.

b Make new friends in class. Walk around and talk to other students. (Use your notes to help you.)

REFLECTION POINT

It isn't important to have lots of friends. But new friends are interesting. Talk to people and make new friends!

››› Workbook, page 29

SPEAKING On the phone

2

Talk on the phone

SPEAK

1 **Look at the photos. Who's got a problem?**

WATCH OR LISTEN

2 1.36 **Watch or listen to the scenes. What is the problem in each phone call?**

A The person's got the wrong number.
B The person's got a long number.
C The person's got a long name.

1
Felix: Hello.
Tara: Hello. Can I speak to your (1) ________ ?
Felix: Sorry, she isn't here.
Tara: OK, (2) ________ she phone me, please? It's Emily Zemontas.
Felix: Er … Can you spell (3) ________ , please?
Tara: Z-E-M-O-N-T-A-S.
Felix: Emily Zemontas. OK.
Tara: Thank you. Goodbye.

2
Kelly: Hi, are you at the cinema?
Felix: (4) ________ , I don't understand.
Kelly: Is that Josh?
Felix: No, it isn't. You've got the wrong (5) ________ .
Kelly: Oh, I'm sorry. Bye.

3
Felix: Hello.
Rico: Is Kyle there?
Felix: No, sorry, he isn't.
Rico: OK. It's Rico. My number is 0703-749031.
Felix: 0703 … Sorry, can (6) ________ repeat that?
Rico: 0703-749031.
Felix: 0703-749031. OK.
Rico: Thanks. Bye.

3 **a** 1.36 **Watch or listen again and complete the conversations.**

b 1.37 **Listen to the sentences and check. Then listen and repeat.**

4 **Work in pairs. Read and practise the conversations in Exercise 2.**

ACT

5 **Work in pairs. Read the situations below. Act the conversations.**

1 Student A: phone Student B.
A: Ask for Student B's father. Your name is Jo Honeycomb.
B: Your father isn't at home. Ask for the person to spell his/her name.
2 Student B: phone Student A.
B: Ask if Student A is at the museum. Ask if it's Ben.
A: You don't understand. It's the wrong number.
3 Student A: phone Student B.
A: Ask for Sam. Your name's Charlie and your number is 765542.
B: Sam isn't at home. Ask Student A to repeat his/her number.

PHRASEBOOK 1.38

Make a call
Can I speak to … ?
Is that … ?
Is … there?
Can he/she phone me, please?

Answer a call
Can you spell that, please?
Sorry, can you repeat that?
Sorry, I don't understand.
You've got the wrong number.
Bye./Goodbye.

Workbook, page 27

WRITING My favourite person

»» Write a description of a person

READD

1 Describe the people in the photos. You can use words from the box.

clever friendly funny grey hair happy nice old small

2 Read Yana's description of her grandmother. Match it to the correct photo. Underline the important words.

Get it right

it's = *it is* (*This is her house. It's very nice.*) OR = *it has* (*It's got a blue door.*)

its = possessive (*This is her house. Its door is blue.*)

1

2

3

Write about your favourite old person.

Babushka Marina, by Yana

My grandma, Babushka Marina, is my dad's mother. She's about 60. She's very clever and friendly. She's got grey hair, very small feet and a small nose. Babushka Marina has got four grandchildren but I'm the only girl. Her house is very nice. It's near our house in Pushchino and its garden's great.

3 Read the tips in the HOW TO box. Then circle the apostrophes in the description in Exercise 2. Are they for missing letters or possessives?

HOW TO

use apostrophes (')

- Use for a missing letter (*you are* = *you're*).
- Use with possessive *'s* or *s'* (*my brother's* eyes, *my two sisters'* eyes).

PRACTISE

4 Read the description. Put in apostrophes.

My brothers 14. Hes got very big feet. My brothers room has got lots of clothes and things everywhere. My two sisters rooms arent like that.

PLAN

5 You're going to write a description of an important person in your life. Use the *Writing plan* to help you prepare.

WRITING PLAN

1 **Choose your person.**
Who is it – family or a friend? How old is he/she? What is his/her face/body like? ☐

2 **Describe his/her things.**
What has he/she got? Describe the things. ☐

3 **Use apostrophes for missing letters and possessives.**
Read the tips in the HOW TO box. ☐

WRITE AND CHECK

6 Write your description. Then check it. Tick (✓) the things in the plan.

SHARE

7 Swap your description with other students. Read their descriptions. Whose description is like yours?

»» Workbook, pages 28–29

VOCABULARY Family

1 Complete the photo description.

SUPERSTAR HAKAN AT HOME

This is my family. Here's my
(1) m________ and
(2) f________. My (3) m______ and
(4) d______ are my number one fans. This is my
(5) g______ m________
and my (6) g______ f________.
I call them (7) G________ and
(8) G________. I'm their only
(9) g________. I'm an
(10) o______ c________ so I haven't
got (11) b________ s or
(12) s________ s.

___ /12

Parts of the body

2 Write the parts of the body from the box.

arm back ear eye face foot
hand head leg mouth nose teeth

HAKAN – FOR YOU!

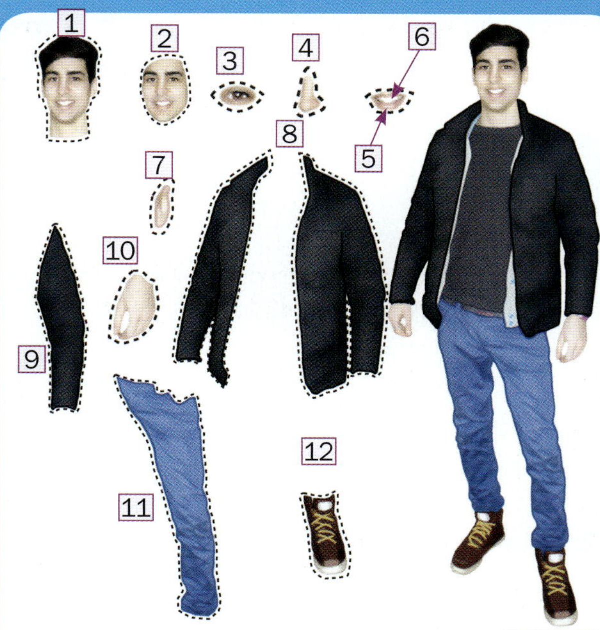

___ /12

GRAMMAR *Have got*

3 Complete the interview with the correct form of *have got*.

Kate: You (1) ________ a cool house. (2) ________ it ________ lots of rooms?

Hakan: Yes, it (3) ________. It (4) ________ ten rooms for my family and me. All the rooms (5) ________ TVs and music players.

Kate: (6) ________ you ________ a special singing room?

Hakan: No, I (7) ________. I sing in all the rooms!

___ /14

Whose?; possessive 's/s' and possessive pronouns

4 Choose the correct options to complete the conversation.

Kate: (1) *Who's* / *Whose* room is this?

Hakan: This is my (2) *mum's* / *mums'* room. Those sunglasses are (3) *hers* / *his*. And this room is (4) *mine* / *yours*. I've got lots of friends – those are all my (5) *friend's* / *friends'* things. These clothes are (6) *ours* / *theirs* too.

___ /12

Your score: ___ /50

SKILLS CHECK

✓✓✓ Yes, I can. No problem!
✓✓ Yes, I can. But I need a bit of help.
✓ Yes, I can. But I need a lot of help.

I can read text messages. ______
I can listen to a quiz show. ______
I can be friendly to other students. ______
I can talk on the phone. ______
I can write a description of a person. ______

Workbook, pages 30–31

READ

1 Complete the five conversations. For each question, choose A, B or C.

Example:

0 *Whose book is this?*

A *It's her.*

B *They're Lucy's.*

(C) *It's mine.*

---

1 *Have you got a brother?*

A *Yes, I have.*

B *Yes, I got a brother.*

C *Yes, one sister.*

2 *Are these your photos?*

A *No, it isn't.*

B *No, they aren't.*

C *Yes, they're yours.*

3 *That's a nice bag.*

A *I can't find it.*

B *It's got the internet.*

C *Thanks. It's new.*

4 *Can you spell your name, please?*

A *P-L-E-A-S-E.*

B *It's P-E-R-E-Z.*

C *Yes, it's Felipe Perez.*

5 *You've got the wrong number.*

A Sorry, I don't know.

B Oh, I'm sorry.

C Sorry, she isn't here.

Reading: ______ /10

EXAM TIPS

answer multiple-choice questions

- Look at the example.
- Read each question. Read the answer choices (A–C).
- Decide which choices are definitely wrong. Look at meaning and grammar to help you.
- Read the question again. Check your answer.

LISTEN

2 1.39 **Listen to a phone call about a drama group. Complete Ivy's notes.**

Drama group

Day:	(0) *Saturday morning*
Number of people in group:	(1) ________
Age of people in group:	(2) ________ years old
Place:	(3) Victoria ________
Name of teacher:	(4) Ms ________
Teacher's phone number:	(5) ________

Listening: ______ /10

EXAM TIPS

listen and complete notes

- Look at the example. It shows you what to do.
- Read the other notes before you listen.
- Decide what type of information you need (names, numbers, …).
- Listen for this information. Write the numbers or words.
- When you listen again, check your answers.

WRITE

3 Read the descriptions and complete the words for parts of the body.

Example:

0 You hear with them. e *a r s*

1 You look with them. e __ __ __

2 They're on your arms. h __ __ __ __

3 They're in your mouth. t __ __ __ __

4 You stand on them. f __ __ __

5 Your nose is on it. f __ __ __

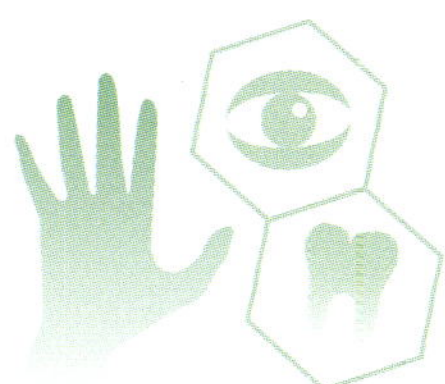

______ /5

EXAM TIPS

complete words from descriptions

- Look at the example. Then look at each question.
- Read the description and the first letter. Can you think of the word?
- Check the number of letters. (One line is one letter.)
- Check your spelling.

4 Read the message from your new friend Basim. Write a reply. Tell Basim about your family (25–35 words).

Tell me about your family. Have you got a big or a small family? Have you got any brothers or sisters? How old are the people in your family? Tell me about them.

Reply

______ /5

Writing: ________ / 10

Progress check score ______ /30

EXAM TIPS

reply to an email or message

- Read the email or message.
- Write your reply. Answer all the questions in the email or message.
- Use the correct number of words.

write a description of a thing
See page 18

use apostrophes (')
See page 28

Download extra speaking activities from the *Beyond* website.

UNIT 3 ANIMAL MAGIC

IN THE PICTURE Adopt a pet

Talk about pets

WORK WITH WORDS Pet animals

1 RECALL **Work in pairs. Look at the photos and write ten parts of the body. You have one minute.**

ear ...

2 a Match the photos (a–j) to the words in the box.

bird ___	cat ___	chicken ___	dog ___	fish ___	hamster ___
horse ___	mouse ___	rabbit ___	sheep ___		

b 1.40 **Listen and check your answers. Then listen and repeat.**

Get it right

one fish, sheep, mouse

two fish, sheep, mice

3 a Read the messages and write animals from Exercise 2a.

b 1.41 **Listen and check your answers.**

4 a 1.42 **Listen to five people talking about their pets. Write the animals from Exercise 2a.**

1 Marta *rabbit*
2 Bryan ___
3 Jacquie ___
4 Leo ___
5 Nicky ___

b 1.42 **Listen again and answer the questions.**

1 Whose pet is called Minnie?
Leo's pet is called Minnie.
2 Whose pet has got big ears?
___
3 Whose pets are blue and green?
___
4 Whose pet hasn't got a name?
___

5 a 1.43 PRONOUNCE **Listen and repeat the short /ɪ/ sound in these words.**

chicken fish rabbit

b 1.44 **Listen and repeat these words.**

Britain six give city sit

adopt a PET

HOME ABOUT US PETS

1 I'm from the United States. I'm five years old. I'm tall and brown, and my name's Hank. I'm a good pet and I'm also a good form of transport. ___

2 I'm Lisa. Please adopt me! I'm one of Britain's favourite pets. I've got two big brown eyes, four legs and a big nose. And I'm yellow. ___

3 My name's Sandra. I'm six months old. I'm a perfect pet because I give you food. Adopt me and eat eggs every day. ___

4 My name's Jimmy and this is my brother, Jock. We're Scottish. I'm black and he's white. We're one year old. ___

5 I'm Dolly. I'm two years and three months old. I don't like the city. I want a home in the country. I've got big ears and a black head. ___

6 **THE MOVING PICTURE** **Watch the video and write the names of the animals you see. Then watch again. How many of the animals are there?**

WRITE AND SPEAK

7 a **Choose a pet from one of the photos in Exercise 2. Give it a new name and complete the form.**

TYPE OF ANIMAL: ....
NAME: ....
COLOUR: ....
DESCRIPTION: ....

b **Work in pairs. Tell your partner about your new pet.**

My pet's a/an …
Its name's …
It's …
It's got …

GO BEYOND

Do the Words & Beyond exercise on page 132.

Workbook, page 32

READING Teach your pet English

Read instructions

SPEAK AND READ

1 Work in pairs. Ask and answer the questions.

1 What pets have you or your friends got?
2 What are their names?

2 1.45 Read the web page. What three things are important to remember?

PHRASE BYTES

I've got … My friend's got … Its name's …

READING TIP

Use pictures to help you understand new words.

TEACH YOUR PET ENGLISH

HOME ABOUT US JOKES CONTACT US

Hi. My name's Harry. How do you do? I can speak English!

Have you got a pet dog, bird or rabbit? Do you speak to your pet in Italian, Japanese or Turkish? Now you can teach your pet English. Use these simple orders and instructions. Don't forget – they aren't for all types of pet.

Here (Come here.)

Sit (Sit down.)
Stay / Wait (Don't move.)

Down (Lie down.)
Up (Stand up.)

Quiet (Be quiet!)
No (Don't do that!)

Here are some more unusual instructions …

Shake (Shake hands.)

Fetch (Find something and come back.)

Remember: always be nice to your pet. Say …
Good boy! / Good girl!

Finally, here are some more things to say to your pet in English:
Hello / Good morning / Good night (+ name of pet)
Walkies! (It's time for a walk.)
Food! (It's time to eat.)

It's important to say the orders in the right way.

CLICK HERE TO LISTEN AND PRACTISE THE ORDERS.

3 Write the orders from Exercise 2 you can probably use with these animals.

1 Bird: *Here …* 2 Cat: 3 Horse:

4 Work in pairs.
Student A: mime an instruction from the web page.
Student B: say the instruction without looking at the page. Then swap roles.

PHRASE BYTES

… are popular pets in …
I speak to my … in …
My dad speaks to …
Animals understand / don't understand me.

REACT

5 Work in pairs. Ask and answer the questions.

1 Are pets popular in your country? Which ones?
2 Do you speak to animals? In which language?
3 Do animals understand you?

GO BEYOND

Write the orders and instructions in the article in your language.

Workbook, page 33

GRAMMAR Imperatives and object pronouns

»» Give orders and instructions

READ AND LISTEN »» Grammar in context

1 a Read the conversation. What pet has Laura got – a horse, a chicken or a hamster?

Mum: Happy birthday, Laura!
Dad: Don't look! OK. Open your eyes.
Laura: Wow, is that for me? A pet .... ! Thanks, Mum. Thanks, Dad.
Mum: Find a quiet place for it.
Laura: Is it a boy or a girl?
Mum: It's a girl.
Dad: Don't put her in your room. They play at night.
Mum: Dad's got a book.
Dad: Yes. It says … give them some food and water every day.
Laura: Yes, Dad.
Dad: And don't forget – pets are for life!

b 1.46 **Listen and check your answer.**

STUDY

2 Complete the examples with words from Exercise 1.

Imperatives

✓ Positive	✗ Negative
Open your eyes.	___Don't___ *look!*
… .... them some food …	*And .... – a pet is for life.*

See GRAMMAR DATABASE, page 122.

3 Complete the table with pronouns from Exercise 1.

Object pronouns

Subject pronouns	Object pronouns
It's a girl.	*Find a quiet place for **it**.*
I	....
you	___you___
he	him
she	....
it	....
we	us
you	you
they	....

See GRAMMAR DATABASE, page 122.

PRACTISE

4 Choose the correct options to complete the sentences.

TIPS ABOUT HAMSTERS

1 *Keep* / *(Don't keep)* your hamster in a hot place.
2 *Be* / *Don't be* nice to it.
3 *Give* / *Don't give* it water and food every day.
4 *Say* / *Don't say* bad things to your hamster.
5 *Play* / *Don't play* with it.
6 *Take* / *Don't take* your hamster to your English class.

5 Match the sentences (1–5) to the signs (a–e) on Laura's walk to school.

1 Don't walk on the grass. ___c___
2 Close the door. ......
3 Please be quiet. ......
4 Don't cross the street. ......
5 Don't play ball games. ......

6 Complete Laura's teacher's instructions. Use object pronouns.

1 'Class, I'm your teacher and I'm talking. Look at ___me___ (your teacher).'
2 'Jack, go to the door and open .... (the door).'
3 'Helen, find some pens and give .... (the pens) to Sanjit.'
4 'Lucas hasn't got his book. Dunya, help .... (Lucas).'
5 'It's Laura's birthday. Let's say 'Happy birthday' to .... (Laura).'
6 'Laura, we've got something for you. Here's a small present from .... (me, your teacher and your classmates).'

SPEAK

7 Work in pairs. Take it in turns to give and follow instructions.

Go to the door.

Give me your pen.

Don't talk.

»» Workbook, pages 34–35

LISTENING AND VOCABULARY A new neighbour

>>> Listen to a description of a room

WORK WITH WORDS Things in your room

1 Work in pairs. Look at the pictures and answer the questions.

1 What animals can you see in the pictures?
2 Which room's your favourite? Why?

PHRASE BYTES

I can see a/an …

Room 1/2 is my favourite because it's got / I like …

Room 1

Room 2

2 a Match the things in the pictures (a–l) to the words in the box.

bed *e*	chair	clock	computer	desk	door .....
floor	light	picture	table	wall	window .....

b 1.47 Listen and check. Then listen and repeat.

3 Write the words from Exercise 2a in the correct category.

Parts of a room: *door, …* **Other things:** *clock, …*
Furniture: *bed, …*

SPEAK AND LISTEN

4 1.48 Listen to the conversation. Which room is it – Room 1 or Room 2?

5 a 1.48 Answer the questions. Then listen again. Compare your answers with a partner.

1 Who's talking – people or pet animals?
2 Who's the new neighbour – a boy, a girl, a cat or a dog?
3 What happens at the end?

b Look at page 141 to check your answers.

6 a Complete the sentences with words from Exercise 2.

'Of course there's a (1) *window* – you're looking in it!'
'There's a small (2) .... next to the bed with a (3) .... on it.'
'There are some (4) .... on the walls. And a (5) ....'
'There are two (6) .... And there's a (7) .... with a computer.'
'Is he there?' – 'Yes! He's on the (8) ....'

b 1.49 Listen and check your answers.

REACT

7 Work in pairs. Ask and answer.

1 What's your favourite TV cartoon?
2 What day's it on TV?
3 Are there any animals in the cartoon? Which ones?

PHRASE BYTES

My favourite TV cartoon's …

It's on … (Saturday/Sunday …)

There's a/an …

GO BEYOND

Do the Words & Beyond exercise on page 132.

Workbook, pages 36–37

GRAMMAR *There is / there are*

Describe a room

READ AND LISTEN Grammar in context

1 1.50 **Read and listen to the conversation. What's wrong with the computer room?**

Natalie: What's your English classroom like?
Mario: It's OK. It's a classroom! There's a table and a chair for the teacher. There are desks for the students. There are some windows. Oh, and there are some pictures of the UK and Australia on the wall.
Natalie: Is there a clock?
Mario: Yes, there is. It's next to the door. Why?
Natalie: The questions are for a school survey. Are there any computers?
Mario: No, there aren't. There are computers in the computer room. I don't like the computer room. There aren't any windows.

STUDY

2 a Complete the table with examples from Exercise 1.

There is / there are	
✓ Positive *There's a/an …* *There are (some) …*	✗ Negative *There isn't a …* *There .... any …*
? Questions *Is there a … ?* Are *there any … ?*	Short answers *Yes, there .... / No, there isn't.* *Yes, there are. / No, there ....*

See GRAMMAR DATABASE, page 122.

b Underline examples of *there is / there are* in Exercise 1.

PRACTISE

3 Look at the photo of Mario's computer room. Are the sentences correct (*C*) or incorrect (*I*)? Rewrite the incorrect sentences.

1 There are some windows. *I*
There aren't any windows
2 There are some brown chairs.
3 There's a clock on the wall.
4 There's one door.
5 There aren't any pictures on the walls.
6 There are three computers.

4 Write questions about your classroom. Then ask and answer them.

1 (a clock) *Is there a clock?*
2 (windows) ....
3 (a table for your teacher) ....
4 (pictures on the wall) ....
5 (a bed) ....
6 (computers) ....

5 Complete the conversation with the correct form of *there is / there are*.

Natalie: What's your room like?
Mario: OK. (1) *There's* a bed and a table.
Natalie: (2) .... a computer on the table?
Mario: No, (3) ....
Natalie: (4) .... any pictures on the walls?
Mario: Yes, there are. (5) .... some pictures of Barcelona Football Club.
Natalie: Is there a window?
Mario: Yes, (6) ....

SPEAK

6 Work in pairs. Complete the tasks.

- Draw a plan of your room and the things in your room. Don't show it to your partner.
- Ask questions about your partner's room. Make a list of his/her things.
- Compare your list with your partner's plan.

Is there a/an … in your room ?
Yes, there is/are.
Are there any … ?
No, there isn't/aren't.

Workbook, page 38

LANGUAGE & BEYOND

Prepare your things for school

SPEAK AND READ

1 a Work in pairs. Look at the pictures for one minute. Then close your books and write the things you remember.

b Open your books and check your lists.

PHRASE BYTES

In picture A there's a notebook …

In picture B there are some …

2 Work in pairs. Which desk is it (A, B or A and B)?

1 It's before school. *A and B*
2 The desk is tidy. ....
3 The homework isn't finished. ....
4 This person's ready for school. ....

DO

3 a Do you usually do these things before bed (A) or before school (B)? Circle your answers.

Do homework	A / B	Ask for bus money	A / B
Prepare clothes for school	A / B	Prepare lunch	A / B
Pack your school bag	A / B	Find keys	A / B

b Where do you usually keep these things – on a table, in your pocket, in your school bag, … ?

school books keys money pens phone

4 Work in pairs. Compare your answers to Exercise 3. When's the best time to do the things in Exercise 3a? Are the places in Exercise 3b good or bad?

REFLECT

5 Talk about the questions. Then read the REFLECTION POINT.

1 When is it good to prepare your school things and do homework?
2 Is it good to keep your school things in one place or different places?
3 Are you ready for school in the morning?

REFLECTION POINT

It's good to prepare your school things and do homework before you go to bed. And it's good to keep your school things in a special place. You can find them quickly and not be late for school.

EXTEND

6 Work in groups. Think of three tips to help students organise their things at school and be ready for each class.

It's good to … / It isn't good to … Keep your things …

PHRASE BYTES

It's good to prepare school things before …

It's good to keep things …

I'm ready / I'm not ready …

SCHOOL SKILLS

Workbook, page 41

SPEAKING You're welcome

Ask for and give things

SPEAK

1 Work in pairs. What can you see in the photos? Describe them.

PHRASE BYTES

There's a … There are some …

WATCH OR LISTEN

2 a Complete the conversations and write the missing words. Use the photos to help you.

1
Kent: Can I have some (1) .... , please?
Poppy: Yes, of course. Here you are.
Kent: Thanks.
Poppy: You're welcome.

2
Jiya: Excuse me. Can I borrow your (2) .... ?
Brett: Sure. Here you are.
Jiya: Thanks.
Brett: You're welcome.

3
Brett: Hi Zac. Can I borrow your (3) .... ?
Zac: No, sorry.
Brett: Oh. OK.
Poppy: You can borrow mine.
Brett: Thanks, Poppy.
Poppy: You're welcome.

b 1.51 Watch or listen to the scenes and check your answers.

3 Complete the sentences with *have* and *borrow*.

1 If you ask to .... something, you don't keep it.
2 If you ask to .... something, you keep it.

4 1.52 Listen and repeat.

5 1.53 Put the sentences in order to make a conversation between Zac and his dad. Then listen and check.

.... Please, Dad!
.... OK. Here you are.
.... No, sorry.
.... Thank you.
.... Dad? Can I have some money?
.... You're welcome.

PHRASEBOOK 1.54

Ask for something
Can I have a/some … , please?
Excuse me. Can I borrow your … ?

Give something
Here you are.

React
Yes, of course.
Sure.
You're welcome.
Thanks.
No, sorry.

ACT

6 Work in pairs. Complete the tasks.

- Prepare two conversations – one at school and one at home.
- Use *borrow* in one conversation and *have* in the other.
- Present your conversations to other students.

Workbook, page 39

WRITING Don't forget

>>> Write a note

READ

1 Match the notes to the pictures.

a

b

c

1

I'm at Grandma's house. There's some pizza in the fridge. Be good. Mum.

2

Don't forget! Give Harry some food and water. There's cat food on the table. Sue.

3

William!! Phone Barbara before 4pm. Basketball practice is at 6pm. Dad.

2 Read the notes again and answer the questions.

1 Where's Mum?
2 What's for lunch?
3 Who or what is Harry?
4 Where's Harry's food?
5 Who is Dad's note for?
6 What time's sports practice?

3 Read the tips in the HOW TO box. Then circle the imperatives in the three notes.

HOW TO

write a note

- Write important information.
- Use imperatives (*Remember / Don't be …*).
- Don't write long sentences.

PRACTISE

4 Underline the important words in these sentences.

1 Class C. Please note: today's German class is in the school hall.
2 Dear Hilary. Enjoy your holiday. Please write and send me a postcard.
3 Don't forget to put the keys on the table for your uncle and aunt.

PLAN

5 You're going to write a note. Use the *Writing plan* to help you prepare.

WRITING PLAN

1 **Choose a person.**
Who's your note for – a member of your family, a friend, a teacher?

2 **Choose a subject for your note.**
What's your note about – a pet animal, food, school?

3 **Prepare your note.**
Read the tips in the HOW TO box.

WRITE AND CHECK

6 Write your note. Then check it. Tick (✓) the things in the plan.

SHARE

7 Swap your note with other students. Who are their notes for?

Workbook, pages 40–41

VOCABULARY Pet animals

1 Write the words for the pets.

1 d ___
2 r ___
3 c ___
4 m ___
5 b ___
6 s ___
7 h ___
8 c ___
9 f ___
10 h ___

___ /10

Things in your room

2 Choose the correct options to complete the text.

Pet Hotel — HOME ABOUT BOOK

All our rooms have four (1) *clocks* / *walls* , a (2) *door* / *floor* (with a special key), a big (3) *bed* / *window* to look at the street and a (4) *floor* / *picture* (if you don't sleep in a bed). There's a big (5) *bed* / *table* to sleep on. There's a small (6) *light* / *table* next to the bed with a (7) *light* / *table* on it. If you want the internet, sit on the (8) *chair* / *computer* at the (9) *desk* / *door* and use the (10) *computer* / *window* . It's free! What time is it? Look at the (11) *clock* / *picture* on the wall. There's also a (12) *table* / *picture* of me on the wall. Have a nice stay!

___ /12

GRAMMAR Imperatives and object pronouns

3 Complete the text with the words and phrases in the box.

come don't forget don't stay eat him them us you

Pet Hotel — HOME ABOUT BOOK

Are you an animal? (1) ___ in a normal hotel. (2) ___ to the Pet Hotel! At the Pet Hotel, we really understand (3) ___ . (4) ___ in the Pet Hotel's famous restaurant. Talk to our chef, Mr Rex, and tell (5) ___ your favourite food. Make new animal friends and relax with (6) ___ in our gardens. (7) ___ the name – *The Pet Hotel*. Call (8) ___ now on 0800-PET-HOTEL!

___ /16

There is / there are

4 Match the sentence halves.

Pet Hotel — HOME ABOUT BOOK

Any questions?

1 Is there ___
2 Yes, ___
3 There's a ___
4 Are there any ___
5 No. There aren't any ___
6 There are some ___

a big garden with lots of grass.
b people at the hotel.
c there is.
d a garden?
e birds, dogs, cats and one elephant.
f people at the Pet Hotel?

___ / 12

Your score: ___ / 50

SKILLS CHECK

✓✓✓ Yes, I can. No problem!
✓✓ Yes, I can. But I need a bit of help.
✓ Yes, I can. But I need a lot of help.

I can read instructions. ___
I can listen to a description of a room. ___
I can prepare my things for school. ___
I can ask for and give things. ___
I can write a note. ___

Workbook, pages 42–43

UNIT 4 PLAY

IN THE PICTURE Free time

>>> Talk about your free-time activities

WORK WITH WORDS Free-time activities

1 RECALL **Work in pairs. Find ten 'free-time' words and phrases. You have three minutes. (Clue: Look at the photos for help.)**

B	H	X	C	I	N	E	M	A	B	T	B
I	S	H	O	P	P	I	N	G	O	E	M
K	E	D	A	V	V	N	P	P	O	L	U
E	T	B	D	B	U	R	B	R	K	E	S
X	F	O	O	T	B	A	L	L	C	V	I
V	I	D	E	O	G	A	M	E	S	I	C
G	C	Y	C	O	I	B	I	N	X	S	K
F	R	I	E	N	D	S	B	B	L	I	W
X	V	V	A	N	P	X	Z	Y	M	O	K
A	R	I	N	T	E	R	N	E	T	N	X

2 2.01 **Work in pairs. Complete the free-time activities with the words in Exercise 1. Listen and check. Then listen and repeat.**

1 go ....
2 go to the ....
3 go on the ....
4 listen to ....
5 meet ....
6 play ....
7 play ....
8 read a ....
9 ride my ....
10 watch ....

3 2.02 **Listen to Jade. Match her free-time activities to the photos (a–j).**

4 THE MOVING PICTURE **Watch the video and write the free-time activities. Then watch again. What countries do you think the people are in?**

a

e

h

j

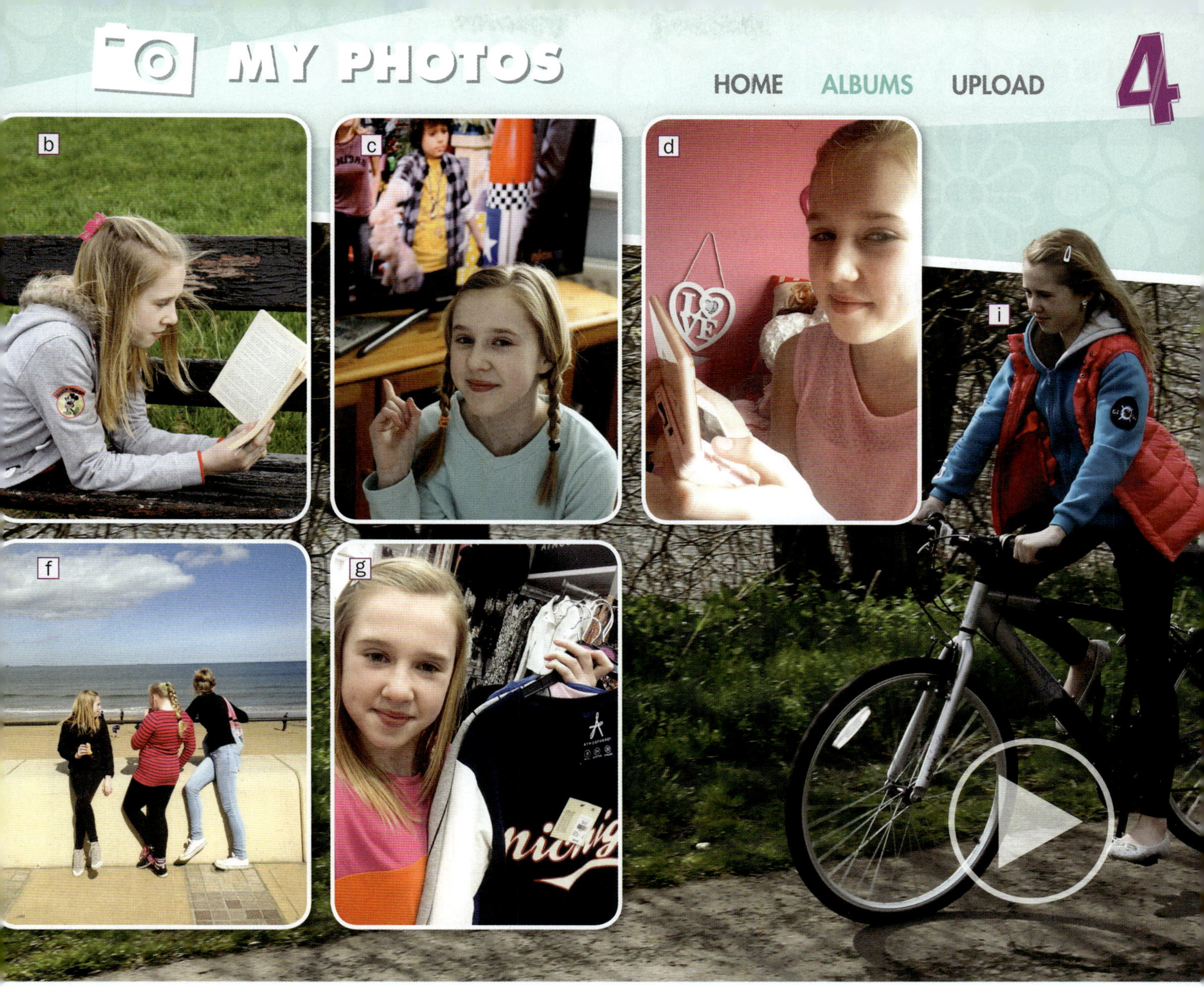

WRITE AND SPEAK

5 a Complete the chart with your top five free-time activities from Exercise 2.

MY TOP FIVE FREE-TIME ACTIVITIES

In my free time I ...	
1	
2	
3	
4	
5	

b Work in pairs. Compare your top five activities.

What's your number one / next activity?

My number two / next activity's ...

That's my ... too.

Really? Mine's ...

GO BEYOND

Do the Words & Beyond exercise on page 133.

READING We can!

Read an article on a website

SPEAK AND READ

1 Work in pairs. Match the disabilities to the pictures.

___ blind ___ deaf ___ in a wheelchair

READING TIP

Before you read a text, think: 'What's it about?' Read the title, headings and first sentences.

2 Look at the website article. Answer the questions.

1 Who's the boy in the photo?
2 Where's he from?
3 What's his disability?

WE CAN! A look at the lives of children with disabilities

Home News Articles About

A message from Jason

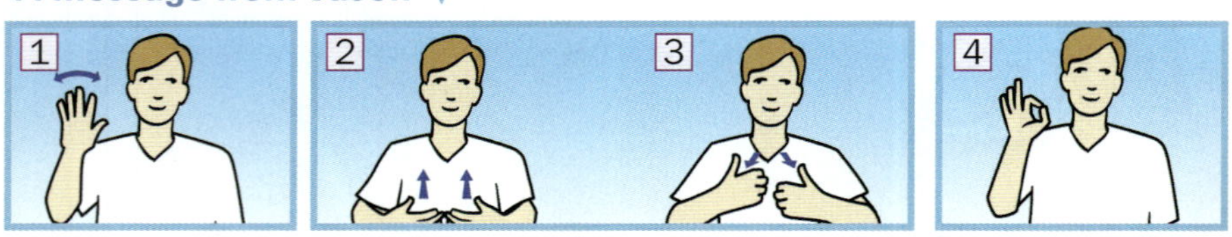

The WE CAN! interview

Name: Jason O'Rourke
Home: Belfast, Northern Ireland

Hi Jason. Can you hear me?
I can, but please sit in front of me.

How much can you hear?
I can't hear in my right ear. In my left ear I'm 50% deaf, but my hearing aid helps.

What's it like for a deaf boy at school?
It's OK. Sometimes people say bad things when they see my hearing aid. They think I can't do normal things. But I can play football, watch TV – all the things they can do.

You write a very popular blog. Why is it popular?
Because when people read it, they can understand my problems. It's not easy for a deaf person in a noisy world.

Can you use sign language?
Yes, I can. I use sign language with a deaf girl at this school.

Can other students understand you?
No, they can't! But they can say 'Hi', 'How are you?' and 'I'm fine' in sign language!

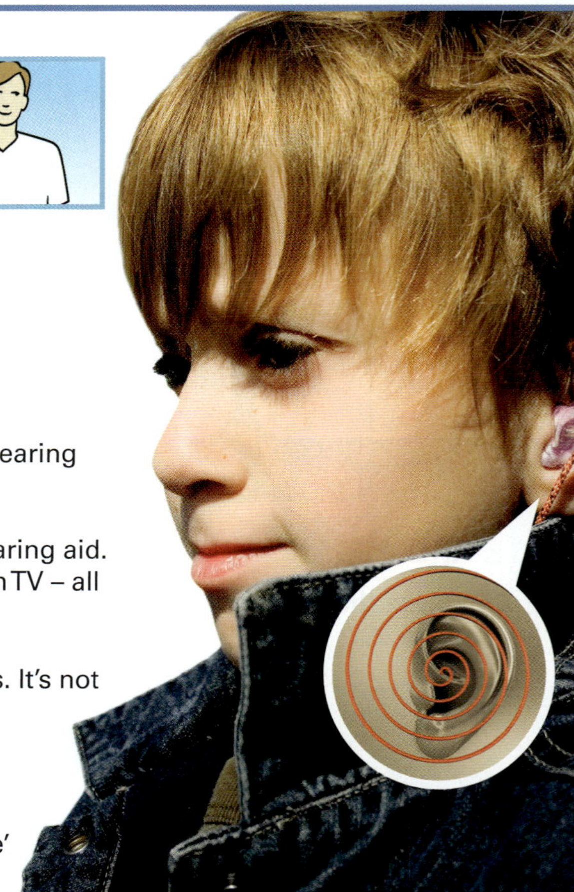

3 (2.03) Read the article. Complete the sentences with TWO words.

1 He's completely deaf in his ______ .
2 There's a ______ in his left ear.
3 Jason's deaf, but he can do ______ .
4 His blog is ______ .
5 The blog's about the life of a ______ in a noisy world.
6 He talks to a deaf girl at his school in ______ .

4 a Look at the pictures in the article. What's Jason saying?

b Work in pairs. Practise the sign language.

PHRASE BYTES

I think it's difficult to hear / listen to …

I think it's difficult when there's a lot of …

REACT

5 Work in pairs. What do you think? Tell your partner.

Jason says, 'It's not easy for a deaf person in a noisy world.' What things are difficult, do you think?

GO BEYOND

Think of another question for Jason. Imagine his answer.

Workbook, page 45

GRAMMAR *Can/can't*

»» Talk about the things you can do

READ AND LISTEN »» Grammar in context

1 2.04 **Read and listen to the conversation. What's Maya's disability?**

Jan: Can you pass me an orange, please?
Maya: I'm sorry, I can't see them.
Jan: Oh! Are you blind?
Maya: Yes, but I can see some things.
Jan: Can you see me?
Maya: Yes, I can, but I can't see your face. Most blind people can see light and dark things. But my teacher's completely blind. She can't see anything.

STUDY

2 Complete the table with ONE word. Then look at Exercise 1 to check.

Can/can't	
✓ **Positive**	✗ **Negative**
I can .... *some things.*	*I can't* .... *your face.*
They can .... *light and dark things.*	*She can't* .... *anything.*
? Questions	**Short answers**
Can you .... *me?*	*Yes, I can.*
	No, she can't.

See GRAMMAR DATABASE, page 123.

PRACTISE

Get it right

I can
you can
he/she/it can

3 Choose the correct options about Maya in Exercise 1.

1 Maya (can) / *can't* see people.
2 She *can* / *can't* watch television.
3 She *can* / *can't* read normal books.
4 She *can* / *can't* listen to audio books.
5 Her teacher *can* / *can't* see people.

4 a Work in pairs. What do you think Mateo can do? Write sentences with *can* and *can't*.

1 swim
2 walk
3 take the bus
4 ride a bike
5 play football
6 play basketball

1 He can/can't ...

b 2.05 **Listen to Mateo and check your answers.**

5 a Put the words in order to make questions.

1 swim? / you / Can
Can you swim?
2 Can / yes in Spanish? / you / say
3 tennis? / Can / play / your teacher
4 people / in New Zealand / English? / Can / speak
5 with your foot? / you / touch your head / Can
6 you and your classmates / for 10 minutes? / be / Can / quiet

b Answer the questions. Use short answers.

1 *Yes, I can. / No, I can't.*

SPEAK

6 Work in groups of three. Ask questions with *can*. Find:

- three things that you can all do.
- one thing that you can do and your partners can't.

Can you ride a bike?

What languages can you speak?

»» Workbook, pages 46–47

LISTENING AND VOCABULARY Are you musical?

Listen to street interviews

WORK WITH WORDS Music

1 2.06 **Match the instruments to the photos. Listen and check. Then listen and repeat.**

...... drums	...... guitar	...... keyboard	...... piano	...... violin

2 a 2.07 **Work in pairs. Listen and match the pieces of music (1–5) to the types of music in the box.**

classical	hip hop	Latin	pop	rock ......

b 2.08 **Listen and check. Then listen and repeat.**

3 a 2.09 PRONOUNCE **Listen and repeat the /p/ sound in *piano*.**

b 2.10 **Listen and repeat these words.**

pronounce repeat hip hop pop

4 **Work in pairs. Ask and answer.**

1 Can you play an instrument? → YES: What instrument? / NO: What instruments do you like?
2 Can you sing or dance?
3 What types of music do you like?

PHRASE BYTES

I can play the ...
I like the ...
I like ... music / hip hop.

LISTEN

5 2.11 **Listen to three interviews in the street. Are the people musical? Write *Yes* or *No*.**

Dora ...... Petra ...... Neil ...... Rianna ......

6 2.11 **Listen again. Complete the sentences with names from Exercise 5.**

1 .... writes songs.
2 .... doesn't like pop music.
3 .... can dance.
4 .... likes classical music.
5 .... likes Latin music.
6 .... and .... play an instrument.

PHRASE BYTES

I think / don't think I'm ...
I'm definitely not ...
I'm not sure.
I can/can't ...

REACT

7 **Work in groups. Are *you* musical? Explain why.**

GO BEYOND

Do the Words & Beyond exercise on page 133.

Workbook, pages 48–49

>>> Talk about habits and routines

READ AND LISTEN >>> Grammar in context

1 2.12 **Read and listen to the interview. What's special about the group?**

TV host: Hello. On today's show we have the Wilsons. Jackie, tell us about your music.

Jackie: Well, we play pop music, but it has a traditional sound too. I play the guitar and I sing. My sister plays the violin. She teaches the violin too. That's my brother Max on keyboards. He writes our songs. And this is a new song. It goes like this …

STUDY

2 Complete the table with examples from Exercise 1.

Present simple

✓ Positive

I, you, we, they

I play *the guitar.*

We .... *pop music.*

he, she, it*: verb + *-s/-es

He writes *our songs.*

My sister .... *the violin.*

go > ....

teach > ....

try > *tries*

have > ....

See GRAMMAR DATABASE, page 123.

PRACTISE

3 Write the verb + *-s, -es* or *-ies*.

	verb	*he/she/it*		verb	*he/she/it*
1	listen	listens	5	practise	....
2	watch	....	6	do	....
3	read	....	7	study	....
4	talk	....	8	arrive	....

4 Complete the descriptions with the verbs in Exercise 3.

The Lateens   home   about   free time

Free time

Carlos is quiet. In his free time he (1) reads a lot of books and he (2) .... to his friends on the internet. He also (3) .... to lots of different types of music – pop, rock, hip hop and classical.

Sofia's mad about music. She (4) .... music at a music school three days a week after school and when she (5) .... home, she (6) .... the piano for hours.

Juan's very active. He (7) .... a lot of different activities in his free time. He's also a big football fan. He (8) .... football matches on television at the weekend.

5 Complete the message with the present simple form of the verbs.

The Lateens   LIKE   FOLLOW

Hi! We're the Lateens and we (1) live (**live**) in Santiago, the capital city of Chile. We (2) .... (**play**) Latin pop music with hip hop influences. My name's Sofia and I'm the singer. I (3) .... (**come**) from a musical family. My mother (4) .... (**teach**) the piano. Carlos (5) .... (**play**) the guitar and keyboard. His guitar hero's Jimmy Hendrix and he (6) .... (**copy**) all his solos. On the drums is Juan. Our group only (7) .... (**have**) three members, so for concerts, we (8) .... (**invite**) other people to play with us.

WRITE AND SPEAK

6 a Work in pairs. Write two or three sentences about a famous group or singer. Don't write their name.

b Work with another pair.

- Tell the other pair about your famous group or singer. (Don't read your sentences.)
- Listen and write the name of the other pair's singer or group.
- At the end, check your answers.

HOMEWORK: LANGUAGE & BEYOND

»» Make a clear note of your homework

SCHOOL SKILLS

SPEAK AND READ

1 Choose the correct option for you. Then compare with a partner.

1 I get ***a little*** / ***a lot of*** homework.
2 I get homework ***two or three*** / ***three or four*** / ***five*** days a week.
3 I do my homework at ***home*** / ***school*** .

2 a Read the lists. Then tick (✓) the things you can see in the picture.

How teachers can give homework:		**How students can make a note of homework:**	
Write it on the board.	......	Make a note on a phone.	......
Tell students.	......	Write it on a piece of paper.	......
Put it on the school website.	......	Write it in a homework diary.	......

b Work in pairs. Ask and answer the questions.

1 How do your teachers give homework?
2 How do you make a note of it?

PHRASE BYTES

Our English teacher writes/tells …
I make a note of it in …
I write it …

DO

3 Work in pairs. Look at the homework diaries above. Then answer the questions.

1 Which homework diary answers these questions (1, 2 or both)?
   a What's the homework? ......
   b What books do I need? ......
   c Where do I write it? ......
   d When's it for? ......
2 Which diary has more information about the homework? ......

PHRASE BYTES

Yes, I can. / No, I can't.
Not always, but …
The best way is to …

REFLECT

4 Talk about the questions. Then read the REFLECTION POINT.

1 Can you always remember your homework?
2 Is your homework always ready on time?
3 What's the best way to make a note of homework? Give details.

REFLECTION POINT

It's important to make a clear note of your homework. Always ask: *What's the task? What do I need? Where do I do it? When's it for?*

EXTEND

5 Make a note of your English homework <u>in English</u>. For help, look again at diary 2 in Exercise 3.

Workbook, page 53

SPEAKING What time is it?

»» Tell the time

SPEAK

1 Work in pairs. Look at the photos. What can you see? Why are Felix and Tara at the theatre?

PHRASE BYTES

In this photo …

I think they're at the theatre because …

What's … in English?

WATCH OR LISTEN

2 2.13 Watch or listen to the scenes. Check your answer to Exercise 1.

1

Kelly: Hi, Felix. What time's the play?
Felix: It's at seven o'clock.
Kelly: I'm sorry, I can't come.
Felix: Don't worry. What time is it now?
Kelly: It's half past five.

2

Felix: Tara? What time is it?
Tara: It's quarter past six. Are you nervous?
Felix: A bit.

3

Felix: Tara? What time is it now?
Tara: It's twenty-five to seven.
Felix: I can hear people.
Tara: Yeah, there are lots of people in the theatre tonight.

4

Felix: Tara? What time is it now?
Tara: It's quarter to seven.
Felix: I can't remember my lines!
Tara: Felix, relax!

3 Read the conversations. Write the times under the clocks.

1 *seven o'clock* 2 ………… 3 ………… 4 ………… 5 …………

4 2.14 Listen and repeat the questions and the times.

5 a Draw clocks with these times. Use Exercise 3 and the picture to help you.

1 It's five o'clock.
2 It's ten to twelve.
3 It's quarter past nine.
4 It's half past eleven.
5 It's quarter to four.
6 It's twenty-five past six.

b Work in pairs.
Student A: close your book.
Student B: point to a clock and ask the time. Repeat for the other clocks. Then swap roles.

PHRASEBOOK 2.15

Ask the time

What time is it?

What time's the … ?

Say the time

It's … o'clock.

It's ten past/to …

It's quarter/half past …

It's quarter to …

It's at …

ACT

6 Work in pairs. Complete the tasks.

- Write a conversation between two people before a film, concert or exam. Include two time questions and two times.
- Practise your conversation. Then present it to other students.

»» Workbook, page 51

WRITING My free time

Write an email

SPEAK AND READ

1 Work in pairs. Circle the correct options for you. Compare your answers.

Survey

1 I write emails. Yes | No

2 Emails are a good way to send messages to:
friends | family | pen friends | classmates | teachers

PHRASE BYTES

Do you write emails?
Yes, I do. I write to ….
No, I don't.
I think emails are a good way to …

2 Read the email. Who's Clara?

New mail | Reply | Forward

Hi Clara,

It's great to have a new pen friend in Argentina. I can't speak Spanish, so we can practise our English. You ask about my free time. Well, I meet my friends, go shopping and go on the internet. On Mondays I have a guitar class. My sister teaches me too. She plays in a group.

Write soon,
Bikem

Get it right

Start an email with:
Hi … / Dear …
Finish with:
Write soon, / Best wishes, …

3 Read the tips in the HOW TO box. Then circle other examples of capital letters in the email.

HOW TO

use capital letters

- Use at the start of a new sentence: *It's great to … .*
- Use for the pronoun 'I': *I have a guitar class.*
- Use for the names of people and places: *Hi Clara.*
- Use for countries, nationalities and languages: *Argentina, Spanish.*
- Use for days of the week: *Monday.*

PRACTISE

4 Rewrite the email with capital letters.

hi bikem,

thanks for your email. it's great to have a pen friend in turkey. is turkish difficult? i think i'm a typical teenager. i meet my friends in my free time too. on saturdays we go to the cinema. at home i listen to music, but i can't play an instrument.

best wishes,
clara

PLAN

5 You're going to write an email to a pen friend. Use the *Writing plan* to help you prepare.

WRITING PLAN

1 **Choose a pen friend.**
Where's your pen friend from? What's his or her name? ☐

2 **Write about your free time.**
What are your free-time activities? Can you play an instrument? ☐

3 **Use capital letters.**
Read the tips in the HOW TO box. ☐

WRITE AND CHECK

6 Write your email. Then check it. Tick (✓) the things in the plan.

SHARE

7 Swap your email with other students. Whose free-time activities are similar to yours?

Workbook, pages 52–53

VOCABULARY Free-time activities

1 Complete the advert with the words in the box.

a book football friends music
my bike shopping television the cinema
the internet video games

THE TLC CLUB
LEARN · PLAY · RELAX

THE QUIET SPACE
read (1) ______
go on (2) ______
THE SPORTS SPACE
play (3) ______
ride (4) ______
THE PLAY SPACE
meet (5) ______
watch (6) ______
play (7) ______
listen to (8) ______
ON SATURDAYS WE GO TO THE CITY CENTRE, WHERE YOU CAN ...
go to (9) ______
go (10) ______

___ /10

Music

2 Complete the words.

THE TLC CLUB
LEARN · PLAY · RELAX

THE LEARN SPACE
YOU CAN LEARN THESE INSTRUMENTS:

1 dr _ _ _
2 gu _ _ _ _
3 ke _ _ _ _ _ _
4 pi _ _ _
5 vi _ _ _ _

AND THESE TYPES OF MUSIC:
6 cl _ _ _ _ _ _ _
7 h _ _ h _ _
8 La _ _ _
9 p _ _
10 r _ _ _

___ /10

GRAMMAR *Can/can't*

3 Complete the interview with *can/can't* and the words in brackets.

Lou: (1) ______ (I/study) music at the TLC?
Piet: Yes, you (2) ______ . We've got a fantastic teacher. She (3) ______ (play) five instruments. (4) ______ (you/play) an instrument?
Lou: No, I (5) ______ . But I want to sing. (6) ______ (she/teach) me to sing?
Piet: Oh, yes. But are you free on Tuesdays or Thursdays? She (7) ______ (not come) on other days.
Lou: I (8) ______ (be) here on Thursdays.
Piet: Great! See you next Thursday then.

___ /16

Present simple

4 Complete the email with the present simple form of the verbs.

New mail Reply Forward

Hi Ursula,
How are you? I've got a new free-time activity! I (1) ______ (go) to singing classes. The teacher's called Helen. She (2) ______ (come) from Russia. She (3) ______ (study) music at the Royal Academy and she (4) ______ (teach) in the evening. We (5) ______ (have) the class on Thursday when school (6) ______ (finish). My friends (7) ______ (want) to have classes too!
Write soon,
Lou

___ /14

Your score: ___ /50

SKILLS CHECK

✓✓✓ Yes, I can. No problem!
✓✓ Yes, I can. But I need a bit of help.
✓ Yes, I can. But I need a lot of help.

I can read an article on a website. ______
I can listen to street interviews. ______
I can make a clear note of my homework. ______
I can tell the time. ______
I can write an email. ______

Workbook, pages 54–55

READ

1 **Read the sentences about Oliver's free time. Choose the best word (A, B or C) for each gap.**

EXAM TIPS

complete sentences with multiple-choice answers

- Look at the example.
- Read each sentence and the choices (A, B or C).
- Decide which words are wrong. For each word, check:
  - Does it have the correct meaning?
  - Can you use it with the words before and after it?
- Read the sentence again. Check your answer.

Example:

0 In the evening I ___ television.
A look B see (C) watch

1 After school I go on the ___ .
A internet B cinema C shopping

2 I listen ___ music on my music player.
A at B with C to

3 My favourite type ___ music is Latin.
A in B of C at

4 I can play the ___ .
A football B piano C video games

5 I ___ my friends at the weekend.
A play B listen C meet

Reading: ______ /10

LISTEN

2 ▶2.16 **Listen to Daria and Luke. What animals or pets have the people in Daria's family got? For questions 1–5, write the correct letter (A–H) next to each person.**

Example:
0 Mum *B*

PEOPLE		PETS
		A bird
1 Dad		B cat
2 her brother		C chickens
3 her sister		D dog
4 Grandma		E mice
5 Grandad		F fish
		G horse
		H hamster

EXAM TIPS

match things in two lists

- Read both lists.
- Listen for the words in the lists.
- Use only five of the words from A–H.

Listening: ______ /10

WRITE

3 **Complete Alice's email to her friend. For questions 1–10, write one word for each space.**

Example:
0 *for*

New mail ← Reply → Forward

Dear Lucia,
Thanks (0) *for* your email about your free time. On school days I (1) ______ homework after school. At the weekend I (2) ______ my bike or I (3) ______ shopping with my mum. I've got (4) ______ dog – her name's Cookie. I take (5) ______ to the park at half (6) ______ seven every morning. She's old and a bit deaf, so she (7) ______'t hear me. But she's a clever dog – she (8) ______ play football! Have you (9) ______ a pet?
(10) ______ soon!
Alice

EXAM TIPS

complete a text with gaps

- First, read the text quickly.
- Look at the words before and after each gap.
- Use only one word in the gap.
- Use the correct form of verbs. Check your spelling.

use capital letters

See page 50.

Writing: ______ / 10

Progress check score ______ /30

UNIT 5

OTHER WORLDS

IN THE PICTURE Welcome to Tomorrowtown

>>> Talk about jobs

WORK WITH WORDS Jobs

1 RECALL **Work in pairs. Write the places. You have two minutes.**

1

f ______

2

f ______ club

3

h ______

4

h ______

5

r ______

6

s ______

7

s ______

8

t ______

2 a Match the people (a–j) in the picture to the places (1–8) in Exercise 1.

1–g

b 2.17 **Listen and check who the people are and where they work.**

3 a Complete the sentences with the jobs in the box.

actor cook doctor farmer football player nurse receptionist shop assistant teacher waiter/waitress

1 'Hi. I'm a(n) ______ . I work at the Tomorrowtown hospital.'
2 'I work at the hospital with the doctor. I'm a(n) ______ .'
3 'Hello. I'm a(n) ______ . You can see me at the Tomorrowtown theatre.'
4 'Welcome to Tomorrowtown Hotel. I'm a(n) ______ at the hotel.'
5 'I'm a(n) ______ . My farm is two kilometres from here.'
6 'I'm a(n) ______ in a clothes shop. There are lots of shops in Tomorrowtown.'
7 'I'm the ______ at Tomorrowtown's Italian restaurant.'
8 'We work at the Italian restaurant. I'm a(n) ______ and he's a(n) ______ .'
9 'I'm a(n) ______ . People come to see me play for Tomorrowtown Football Club.'
10 'I'm a(n) ______ at Tomorrowtown High School. I teach all the kids in Tomorrowtown.'

b 2.18 **Listen and check. Then listen and repeat.**

Get it right

I'm a doctor.

I'm an actor.

4 a ▶2.19 PRONOUNCE **Listen and repeat the /ə/ sound in these words.**

doct<u>or</u> farm<u>er</u> teach<u>er</u>

b ▶2.20 **Find three more jobs in Exercise 3 with the /ə/ sound. Then listen and check.**

5 THE MOVING PICTURE ▶ **Watch the video about Tomorrowtown. Which job in Exercise 3a is NOT in the video?**

SPEAK

6 **Work in pairs. Read and follow the Tomorrowtown instructions.**

Hi. My name's … I'm a/an …

Hello, Alex. I'm … I'm a/an …

I work in …

7 **Introduce yourself to other students in the class. What are their jobs? Which is the class's favourite job?**

WELCOME TO
TOMORROWTOWN

1 Look at the Tomorrowtown people. Choose a person. *Tip:* Choose a different person from your partner.
2 Make notes about your person. *Tip:* Answer these questions – *What's your name? What's your job?*
3 Introduce yourself to your partner.

GO BEYOND

Do the Words & Beyond exercise on page 134.

Workbook, page 56

Read a questionnaire

SPEAK AND READ

1 Work in pairs. Ask and answer.

1 How old are you? What do you do?
2 Go 15 years into the future … How old are you? What do you do?

2 2.21 Read the instructions for the questionnaire. Decide if the sentences are correct (*C*) or incorrect (*I*). Correct the incorrect sentences.

1 The questionnaire is to find the perfect job for you. ____
2 For each question, you can choose one or two answers. ____
3 You tick (✓) the answers you choose. ____
4 When you finish, you count your answers (A, B or C). ____
5 If your answers are 1A, 2C and 3A, you read the section *Mostly As*. ____

3 Do the questionnaire and read your results.

PHRASE BYTES

I'm … years old.
I'm a/an …
How do you say … in English?

READING TIP

It's important to read instructions slowly and carefully.

My perfect job

Instructions

Do this questionnaire and find your perfect job of the future! Read each question and choose **one** of the answers A, B or C. Circle your answer. Then count the number of A, B or C answers and read about your perfect job.

1 Which of these free-time activities do you do?
A I meet friends or go shopping.
B I play football or ride a bike.
C I go to the cinema or read a book.

2 Which musical instrument do you want to play?
A I want to play the guitar in a pop group.
B I want to play the drums.
C I want to play the piano and sing.

3 Do you play games?
A Yes, I do. I play video games with my friends.
B Yes, I do. I play ball games – football, basketball …
C No, I don't. I like to make things.

Mostly As
You like people. Your perfect job's a doctor, nurse, shop assistant or receptionist.

Mostly Bs
You're an active person. Your perfect job's a farmer or football player.

Mostly Cs
You like to create. Your perfect job's an actor, cook or teacher.

4 Add *waiter/waitress* to one of the groups. Which group is most suitable (A, B or C)?

REACT

5 Work in pairs. Ask and answer the questions.

1 Do you agree with the results of the questionnaire?
2 Is your perfect job in the questionnaire?
3 Do you like questionnaires? Why?/Why not?

PHRASE BYTES

The questionnaire says …
I agree. / I don't agree.
My perfect job's a/an …
I like / don't like questionnaires. They're fun/boring.

GO BEYOND

Write another question for the questionnaire and three possible answers.

Workbook, page 57

GRAMMAR Present simple

»» Ask and answer questions about habits and routines

READ AND LISTEN »» Grammar in context

1 a Read the questions and answers. Where does the mystery person work? What's her job?

Q: Does the mystery person work on a farm?
A: No, she doesn't.
Q: Does she work in a school?
A: Yes, she does. But she doesn't teach.
Q: Do students see her every day?
A: Yes, they do.
Q: What time does she start work?
A: I don't know.
Q: Do people ask her for things?
A: Yes, they do.
Q: What do they ask her for?
A: They ask her for food.
Q: Is she a ______ ?
A: Yes, she is!

b 2.22 **Listen and check.**

STUDY

2 Complete the table with examples from Exercise 1.

Present simple	
✓ **Positive** *I know.* *She teaches.*	✗ **Negative** *I **don't** know.* *She ______ teach.*
? **Questions** ***Do** you know the answer?* ______ *in a school?* Do *people ask her for things?* ______ *does she start work?* ______ *do they ask her for?*	**Answers** *Yes, I **do**. / No, I **don't**.* *Yes, she **does**. / No, she ______ .* *Yes, ______ . / No, they **don't**.* *I don't know.* *They ask her for food.*

See GRAMMAR DATABASE, page 124.

Get it right

She works … She doesn't work … Does she work … ?

Workbook, pages 58–59

PRACTISE

3 a Complete the sentences with the correct form of the verbs.

ask buy do give help smile watch ~~work~~

1 I work with animals.
2 People ______ things from me.
3 The waiter ______ my food to people.
4 You ______ me play football.
5 I ______ people.
6 Your teacher ______ the same job.
7 We ______ : 'Would you like to order now?'
8 I ______ at people in a hotel.

b 2.23 **Make the sentences negative. Listen and check. Then identify the mystery job.**

1 *I don't work with animals.*

4 Complete the conversation with *do*, *don't*, *does* and *doesn't*.

Mollie: (1) Do you know Jenny?
Jane: No, I (2) ______ .
(3) ______ she go to our school?
Mollie: Yes, she (4) ______ . She says her mum and dad are famous.
Jane: Really? What (5) ______ they do?
Mollie: Her dad's a football player and her mum's an actor.
Jane: Wow! Who are they?
Mollie: I (6) ______ know. It's a mystery.
Jane: (7) ______ you believe her?
Mollie: Yes, I (8) ______ .
Jane: Really?

5 Write questions about a mystery person.

1 play / football / the mystery person?
Does the mystery person play football?
2 Where / live / the mystery person?
______
3 What / do / the mystery person?
______
4 you / know / the mystery person?
______

SPEAK

6 Work in pairs.

- **Student A: look at page 141. Student B: look at page 142. Choose one of the people. Don't tell your partner.**
- **Ask and answer the questions in Exercise 5.**
- **Can you guess the name of your partner's mystery person?**

Is the mystery person a man or a woman?

She's a woman. / He's a man.

LISTENING AND VOCABULARY My daily routine

››› Listen to a radio show

WORK WITH WORDS Daily activities

1 a Work in pairs. Match the daily routine activities to the icons.

do my homework	finish school	get up	go home .....
go to bed	go to school	have a shower	have breakfast .....
have dinner	have lunch		

b ▶2.24 Listen and check. Then listen and repeat.

2 Put the activities in Exercise 1 in order for your day. Then compare with a partner.

First I … *Then I …* *Next I …*

SPEAK AND LISTEN

3 Work in pairs. Describe the pictures.

1 A B C
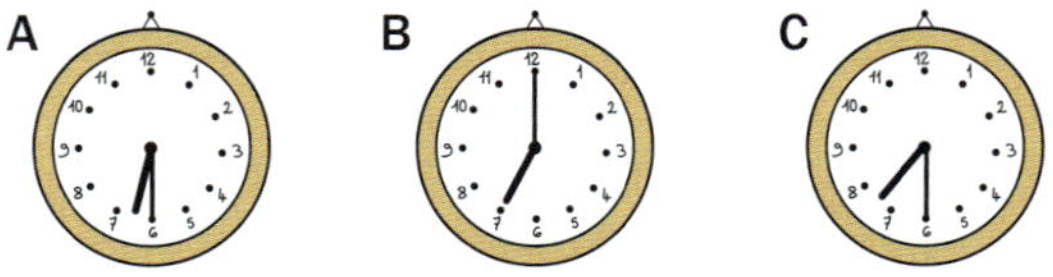

2 A B C / 3 A B C
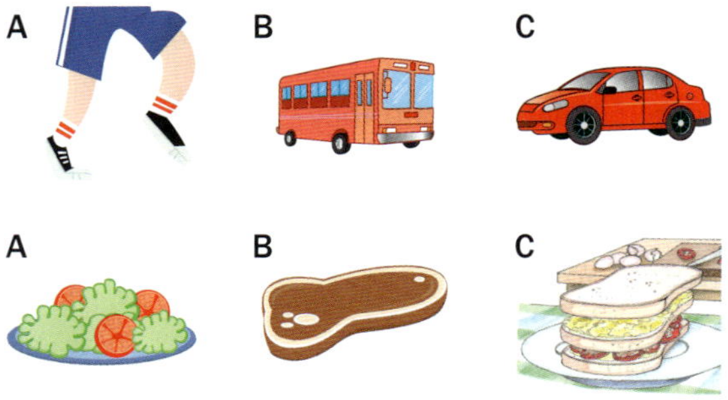

4 A B C / 5 A B C
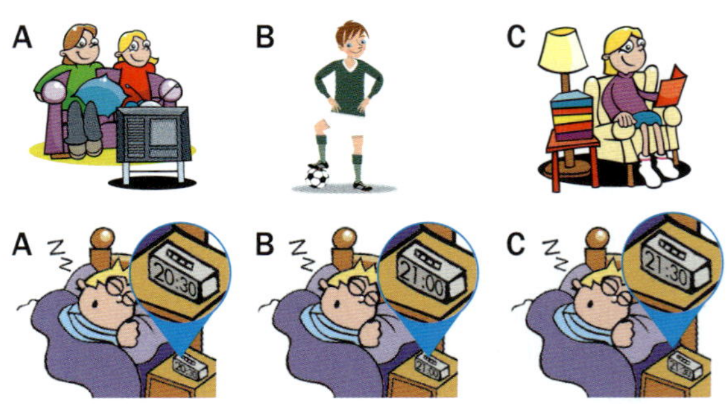

PHRASE BYTES

In picture A the time's …
There's a …
I can see …

4 ▶2.25 Listen to the radio show. What does Daniel's mum do? Where does she work?

5 a ▶2.25 Listen again. Read the questions and choose the correct picture (A, B or C).

1 What time does Daniel get up?
2 How does he go to school?
3 What does he have for lunch?
4 What does he do after school?
5 When does he go to bed?

b Write five sentences about Daniel.

He gets up at …

PHRASE BYTES

Daniel gets up at … I get up at …
School starts at …
My mum/dad goes to work at …

REACT

6 Work in pairs. Ask and answer the questions.

1 Is Daniel's daily routine the same as yours? What's different?
2 When does school start and finish in your country?
3 Does your mum or dad work? When does she/he work?

GO BEYOND

Do the Words & Beyond exercise on page 134.

››› Workbook, pages 60–61

GRAMMAR Adverbs of frequency

Say how often you do things

READ Grammar in context

1 **Read the survey and Holly's answers. What does she do in the evening?**

WHAT'S YOUR DAILY ROUTINE?
ANSWER THE QUESTIONS IN OUR SURVEY.

WHAT TIME DO YOU USUALLY GET UP?
My mum and dad are farmers. So I **often** get up at 5 to help them and give food to the animals.

HOW DO YOU GO TO SCHOOL?
I **usually** go to school by bus. My dad **sometimes** takes me by car.

HOW OFTEN DO YOU HAVE LUNCH AT SCHOOL?
I **always** have lunch at school. I can't go home.

AND WHAT DO YOU DO AFTER SCHOOL?
I **usually** go home and do my homework. My dad doesn't like TV so I **never** watch it at home. I usually read a book. Then I go to bed at around 9 o'clock.

STUDY

2 **Complete the table with examples from Exercise 1.**

Adverbs of frequency

I ___often___ ***get up** at 5.*
I ________ ***have** lunch at school.*

? Questions
What time do you ________ ***get up**?*
How ________ *do you have lunch at school?*

See GRAMMAR DATABASE, page 124.

3 **Complete the line with the adverbs. Use Exercise 1 to help you.**

never   often

100% |______|______|______|______| 0%

always   usually   ________   sometimes   ________

PRACTISE

4 **a** **Write the sentences with the adverbs of frequency in the correct place.**

1 I get up at 07:00. (usually)
I usually get up at 07:00.
2 I have a shower before breakfast. (always)
____
3 I go to school by bus. (often)
____
4 I read a book after dinner. (sometimes)
____
5 I go to bed before 21:00. (never)
____

b **Which of the sentences are true for you?**

5 **Write true sentences for you, your friends and family. Use adverbs of frequency.**

1 eat / chocolate
My brother often eats chocolate.
2 go / to the cinema
3 play / football at the weekend
4 drink / coffee
5 go / to school by bus
6 watch / TV before school

6 **Circle the correct option.**

Marta: Hi Simon! Do you (1) *often* / *never* come to school by bus?
Simon: No, I don't. My mum (2) *never* / *usually* takes me by car on her way to work.
Marta: What does she do?
Simon: She's a teacher. She (3) *usually* / *never* starts work at 8.30 but she (4) *always* / *sometimes* works at home. How often do you get the bus?
Marta: I (5) *always* / *never* get the bus. I don't live near the school and my mum doesn't drive so I (6) *never* / *sometimes* come by car.

7 **Do the survey.**

HOW OFTEN DO YOU DO THESE THINGS? TICK (✓) THE CORRECT BOX.	0%	30%	60%	80%	100%
1 PLAY VIDEO GAMES					
2 GO SHOPPING					
3 GO ON THE INTERNET					
4 LISTEN TO MUSIC					
5 GET UP LATE					
6 READ A BOOK					

SPEAK

8 **Work in pairs. Ask and answer the questions in Exercise 7. Use adverbs of frequency.**

How often do you play video games?

I often play video games. And you?

I sometimes play them.

Workbook, page 62

LANGUAGE & BEYOND

HELP! HOW OFTEN DO YOU NEED HELP TO ...

	OFTEN	SOMETIMES	NEVER
UNDERSTAND SOMETHING IN CLASS?			
DO HOMEWORK?			
FIND SOMETHING (CLOTHES, KEYS, ...)?			
USE SOMETHING (A COMPUTER, THE INTERNET, ...)?			

»» Ask for help

SPEAK AND READ

1 **Work in pairs. Describe the situation in the photo above.**

2 **Work in pairs. Look at the boy at the back on the left. Why doesn't he know the answer to the question? Tick (✓) the possible answers.**

- ...... He hasn't got his books.
- ...... He's a new student.
- ...... He doesn't understand the question.
- ...... He can't hear the teacher.

PHRASE BYTES

It's a classroom.

There's a ...

There are some ...

DO

3 **a** **Do the HELP! survey above.**

b **Who do you usually ask for help in the situations in the survey – your teacher, mum, dad, classmate, friend, brother, sister, ... ? Why?**

4 **Work in pairs. Compare your answers to Exercise 3.**

I often need help to do my homework.

I sometimes need help. Who do you ask for help?

I usually ask my big brother because ...

5 **Work in pairs. Match phrases 1–4 to the situations in Exercise 3a.**

1 'Mum? Can you help me with this exercise?'
2 'Can you show me how to play this game?'
3 'Can you repeat the question, please?'
4 'I can't find my school bag. Can you help me find it?'

REFLECT

6 **Talk about the questions. Then read the REFLECTION POINT.**

1 Why is it good to ask for help?
2 Who do you ask for help in class and at home?
3 What phrases can you use to ask for help?

PHRASE BYTES

It's good to ask for help because ...

At home / In class I usually ask ...

You can say ...

EXTEND

7 **Work in groups. Choose one of the situations in Exercise 3a and prepare a scene. Then present it to other students.**

REFLECTION POINT

It's important to ask for help if you don't understand something. In class ask the teacher or other students. At home, ask your family.

SCHOOL SKILLS

»» Workbook, page 65

SPEAKING Why not?

Ask for and give reasons

SPEAK

1 **Work in pairs. Look at the photos of Becca and Zac and describe the situation.**

PHRASE BYTES

Becca's got a school book.

Maybe she …

I think Zac's her brother/father …

WATCH OR LISTEN

2 2.26 **Watch or listen to the scene. Why can't Becca do her homework?**

Becca: Dad? Are you busy?
Dad: No. Why?
Becca: Because (1) ………………………… .
Dad: OK.
Becca: Can I go and see Kelly?
Dad: No.
Becca: Why not?
Dad: Because (2) ………………………… .
Becca: I can't do my homework.
Dad: Why not?
Becca: Because (3) ………………………… .
Dad: Give it to me.
Becca: Why?
Dad: Because (4) ………………………… .
Becca: OK. Here you are.
Dad: Ah. Where's your mother?
Becca: Why?
Dad: Because …

3 a Put the words in order to make phrases.

1 task / understand / don't / I / the ………………………………
2 homework / got / you've ………………………………
3 help / I / you / can / maybe ………………………………
4 you / I / question / ask / want / to / a ………………………………

b Complete the conversation in Exercise 2 with the phrases.

4 2.26 **Watch or listen again and check your answers. Then complete the last line of the conversation in your own words.**

Get it right

I can't do my homework.

Why not?

5 Match the questions to the reasons.

1 Why are you happy?
2 Why do you want to be a farmer?
3 Why isn't your sister here?
4 Why do we do homework?

a Because she's at the cinema.
b Because we need to practise.
c Because I like animals.
d Because it's Saturday.

ACT

6 **Work in pairs. Complete the tasks.**

- Read the first lines of the conversations.
  - *- How do you usually go to school?*
  - *- Who's your favourite football player?*
  - *- Do you like classical music?*
  - *- Mum? Can I go to the cinema?*
- Continue the conversations with *why* and *because*.
- Practise the conversations.
- Present one of your conversations to other students.

PHRASEBOOK 2.27

Ask for reasons

(*Give it to me.*)

Why?

(*I can't do my homework.*)

Why not?

Give reasons

Because I/you/it …

Workbook, page 63

>>> Write a website post

SPEAK AND READ

1 Work in pairs. Tick (✓) the things you do on a school day. How often do you do them? Compare your answers with your partner.

get up late
have a sandwich
do homework
chat with friends
watch TV
ride a bike

2 Read the website post. Which of the things in Exercise 1 does Sally do?

Get it right

We don't have free school meals in Australia.

We = me + all the other schoolchildren in Australia

ASK ANY QUESTION

Home | Technology | Health | Sports | History | World

Q: What's a normal school day for kids in Australia?

In Australia we usually get up at 7 and have breakfast. School starts at 9 o'clock. We have lunch at 1 but we don't have free school meals in Australia. I often have a sandwich. I finish school at 3. Then I go home and do my homework. I usually go to bed at 9 but I sometimes watch television.

Sally G. Australia

3 Read the tips in the HOW TO box. Then underline examples of *and* and *but* in the website post.

HOW TO

use *and* and *but*

- Use *and* to add another similar idea.
- Use *but* to add a different idea.

PRACTISE

4 Use *and* or *but* to join the sentences.

1 I like ice cream. I don't like chocolate ice cream.
I like ice cream but I don't like chocolate ice cream.
2 My sister doesn't play an instrument. She loves music.
3 There's a clock on the wall. There are some pictures.
4 On Sundays we usually go to the cinema. We have dinner at a restaurant.
5 I usually go to bed at 9. On Saturdays I go to bed at 10.
6 They don't have free school meals in Australia. We have free school meals here.

PLAN

5 You're going to write a website post about a normal school day in your country. Use the *Writing plan* to help you prepare.

WRITING PLAN

1 **Make a list of things you do on a school day.**
What do you do? How often do you do them?

2 **Include information about your country.**
Which things are true for all the schoolchildren in your country (*we*)?

3 **Use *and* and *but*.**
Read the tips in the HOW TO box.

WRITE AND CHECK

6 Write your website post. Then check it. Tick (✓) the things in the plan.

SHARE

7 Swap your website post with other students. Are they similar? What's different?

Workbook, pages 64–65

VOCABULARY Jobs

1 Write the jobs.

MEET YOUR ME2! YOUR ME2 CAN …

1 work in a shop. ....
2 help students learn things. ....
3 take people's food to their restaurant table. ....
4 work in a theatre. ....
5 make food in a restaurant. ....
6 help people in a hospital. ....
7 help the doctor at the hospital. ....
8 work with animals. ....
9 play football. ....
10 welcome people to a hotel. ....

___ /10

Daily activities

2 Complete the daily routine phrases with the verbs in the box.

does finishes gets goes (x3) has (x4)

FOLLOW THE DAILY ROUTINE OF YOUR ME2!

Me2 (1) .... up at 5 o'clock every day. It (2) .... a shower and then it (3) .... breakfast. Me2 (4) .... to school on foot. It (5) .... lunch at school (a special Me2 sandwich). Me2 (6) .... school at 3.30. After school it (7) .... home and (8) .... its homework. It (9) .... dinner at 7.30 and (10) .... to bed at 9.00.

___ /10

GRAMMAR Present simple

3 Choose the correct options to complete the conversation.

ME2 HOME FAQ ABOUT

Q: (1) *Do* / *Does* I need the internet to use Me2?
A: Yes, you (2) *do* / *don't*. First you register on the website. Then you choose a name and a job for your Me2.
Q: (3) *Do* / *Does* other people see my personal information?
A: No, they (4) *don't* / *doesn't*. They only see your Me2 information.
Q: How much (5) *do* / *does* it cost?
A: It (6) *don't* / *doesn't* cost anything. It's free!
Q: (7) *Do* / *Does* Me2 sleep?
A: Yes, it (8) *do* / *does*.

___ /16

Adverbs of frequency

4 Rewrite the sentences. Write an adverb of frequency from the box in the correct place in each sentence.

always (x2) never (x2) often sometimes usually

1 How do you visit the Me2 website?
2 I visit it in the morning after breakfast. (100%)
3 I visit the website at school because my teacher doesn't like it. (0%)
4 Me2 is happy to see me. (100%)
5 We talk about football. (80%)
6 We play video games. (30%)
7 But I win! (0%)

___ /14

Your score: ___ /50

SKILLS CHECK

✓✓✓ Yes, I can. No problem!
✓✓ Yes, I can. But I need a bit of help.
✓ Yes, I can. But I need a lot of help.

I can read a questionnaire. ....
I can listen to a radio show. ....
I can ask for help. ....
I can ask for and give reasons. ....
I can write a website post. ....

Workbook, pages 66–67

TOP TENTS

6 UNIT HOLIDAY HOME

IN THE PICTURE Our holiday home

»» Talk about homes

WORK WITH WORDS Homes

1 RECALL **Work in pairs. Complete the things in a room with *a, e, i, o* and *u*. You have two minutes.**

1 b ___ d
2 ch ___ ___ r
3 cl ___ ck
4 c ___ mp ___ t ___ r
5 d ___ sk
6 d ___ ___ r
7 fl ___ ___ r
8 l ___ ght
9 p ___ ct ___ r ___
10 t ___ bl ___
11 w ___ ll
12 w ___ ndow

2 a 2.28 **Listen. Where does Oscar live? Choose the correct place.**

A flat/apartment with swimming pool

B flat/apartment with big balcony

C house with garden

Get it right
flat = British English
apartment = American English

b 2.29 **Listen and repeat the words under the photos.**

3 **Look at the plan and the photos of Oscar's holiday home. What sort of holiday home is it? How many rooms has it got?**

PHRASE BYTES
It's an apartment / a hotel / a tent / a house …
It's got …

4 a 2.30 **Listen. Write the correct words from the box for 1–6 on the plan.**

bathroom	bedroom	dining room	hall	living room	kitchen

b 2.31 **Listen and check. Then listen and repeat.**

5 Write the correct words from exercises 2 and 4.

1 You eat in this room. ________
2 You sleep in this room. ________
3 You swim here. ________
4 You wash here. ________
5 You cook in this room. ________
6 You sit outside here. ________ / ________
7 You sit or watch TV or talk in this room. ________
8 You come in or go to other rooms here. ________
9 You live here in a big city. ________ / ________
10 This has often got more rooms than 9. ________

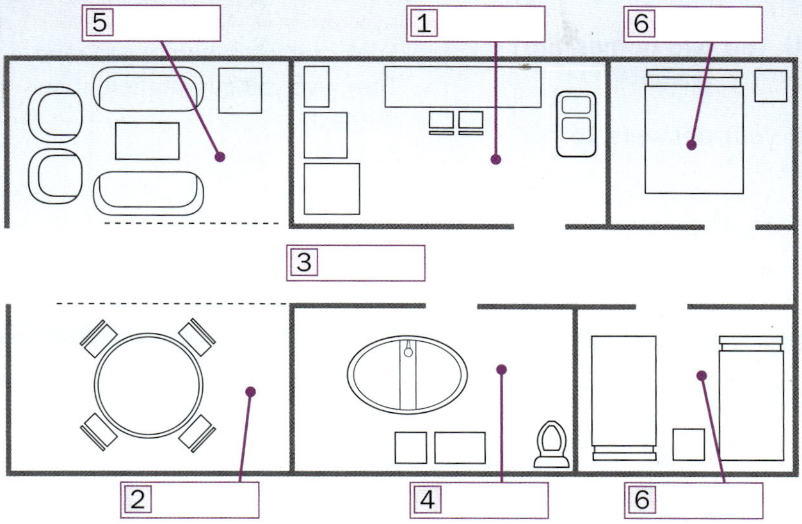

6 **THE MOVING PICTURE** **Watch the video. What does Oscar do on holiday?**

SPEAK

7 a **Draw a plan of your home. Don't write the names of the rooms.**

b **Work in pairs. Ask and answer about your homes.**

I live in a house/flat.

What room's that?

That's the living room / my parents' bedroom / my room ...

Have you got a balcony / garden / swimming pool?

Yes, we have. / No, we haven't.

GO BEYOND

Do the Words & Beyond exercise on page 135.

Workbook, page 68

READING Home from home

Read chat messages

READ

1 **Look at the photos. Where do you think the two homes are? What are the places like?**

2 2.32 **Read the chat messages. Check your answers to Exercise 1 and complete the sentences.**

1 Josina usually lives in ………… .
2 Kasem usually lives in ………… .
3 Now, Josina is in ………… and Kasem is in ………… – because they're on a house ………… .

READING TIP

Look at photos before you read. They give you information about the text.

BEYOND INSTANT MESSENGER — PROFILES SETTINGS FRIENDS

JOSINA: Hi Kasem. Is everything OK there? We're in your home! I love it! I love your room – your bed's more comfortable than mine!
KASEM: I love your houseboat! Your home is really cool.
JOSINA: Is it your first time in Europe?
KASEM: Yes, it is. I like the Netherlands. It's quieter than at home. And it's very clean.
JOSINA: It's my first time in Asia too. Bangkok is much bigger and noisier than Amsterdam. It's exciting here!
KASEM: Do you like the view from the apartment?
JOSINA: Yes, it's fantastic. All those tall buildings!
KASEM: A house swap is a great idea. It's more interesting than a boring, expensive hotel. I don't like hotels.
JOSINA: Really? I love hotels. My parents are terrible cooks. Hotel food is better than their cooking. Oh … it's half past six – time for dinner.
KASEM: Right – it's five hours later in Thailand. It's time for lunch here.

ABC — YOUR MESSAGE | — SEND

3 **Read the messages again. Choose the correct answer (A, B or C).**

1 Josina …
 A thinks Kasem's home is OK. B doesn't think his bed is comfortable. C likes Kasem's room.
2 This is Kasem's …
 A first visit to Asia. B first visit to Europe. C first time on a boat.
3 The apartment in Bangkok …
 A has got a great view. B is very quiet. C is like a hotel.
4 Kasem thinks a house swap is …
 A OK. B interesting. C a bad idea.
5 Josina likes hotels because her parents …
 A always stay in hotels. B make great food. C can't cook.
6 In Amsterdam the time is …
 A 18:30. B 13:30. C 23:30.

PHRASE BYTES

We go to …
My favourite house swap home is a/an …
A … is better than … because …

REACT

4 **Work in pairs. What do you think? Tell your partner.**

1 Your parents want to do a house swap. Where do you go?
2 What sort of home do you choose for your swap?
3 Is a house swap better than a hotel? Why?/Why not?

GO BEYOND

Underline all the adjectives (*OK, comfortable, …*) in the text.

Workbook, page 69

GRAMMAR Comparative adjectives

»» Compare two places, people or things

READ AND LISTEN »» Grammar in context

1 (▶2.33) **Read and listen to the conversation. Which city is more popular – New York or Washington? Why?**

Grace: What's the capital city of the USA?
Lola: New York.
Grace: No! It's Washington DC. A lot of people think New York's the capital because it's bigger and more famous than Washington. Washington is smaller and quieter.
Lola: Oh. But New York is cooler! It's in a lot of American films.
Grace: This website says New York is dirtier, more dangerous and more expensive than Washington. But New York is more popular because the shops and restaurants are better.

STUDY

2 Complete the table with examples from Exercise 1.

Comparative adjectives	
short adjective + *-er*	*smaller* , ... *bigger*, ...
more + long adjective	*more famous* *more dangerous* ....
irregular adjectives	good > .... bad > *worse* far > *further*

See GRAMMAR DATABASE, page 125.

3 Complete the sentences with the correct word.

1 New York's bigger .... Washington.
2 New York's dirtier .... Washington.

PRACTISE

4 Complete the sentences with the correct form of the comparative.

1 **Brazil**: Are people *richer* (**rich**) in Rio de Janeiro than in Brasilia?
2 **Australia**: Canberra is .... (**far**) from the beach than Sydney.
3 **Canada**: Toronto is .... (**expensive**) than Ottawa.
4 **Switzerland**: Geneva is .... (**interesting**) than Bern.
5 **Turkey**: Ankara is .... (**cheap**) than Istanbul.
6 **Morocco**: Rabat is .... (**old**) than Casablanca.

5 a Compare the two holiday places. Write six sentences with the adjectives.

HOLIDAY REVIEWS

A  B 

	Wonderville	Superville
1 safe	★★★★★	★★★☆☆
2 clean	★★★★☆	★★★★★
3 new	★★★☆☆	★★★★★
4 friendly	★★★★★	★☆☆☆☆
5 interesting	★★★★☆	★★★☆☆
6 good holiday place	★★★★★	★★★☆☆

1 *Wonderville is safer than Superville.*

b Compare two towns or places in your country. Write three to five sentences.

SPEAK

6 Work in pairs. Student A: look at page 141. Student B: look at page 142.
Find out which trip is:
– longer ....
– more expensive ....
– more comfortable ....
– more interesting ....

My trip is for … days.

My trip is for … Mine's shorter/longer.

I think my/your trip's more interesting because …

LISTENING AND VOCABULARY Favourite food

Understand a conversation about food

WORK WITH WORDS Food and drink

1 a Work in pairs. What food and drinks can you remember from Units 1–5. Make a list.

b Answer the questions about your list.

1 Which things are food?
2 Which things are drinks?
3 Which things are fruit?

2 a 2.34 Look at more food and drinks. Listen to Corey. Match the words to the photos.

bread ___	cheese ___	chicken ___	egg ___
juice ___	meat ___	milk ___	oil ___
pasta ___	rice ___	steak ___	vegetables ___

a

b

c

d

e
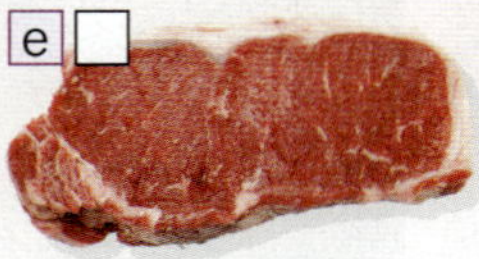
f

g
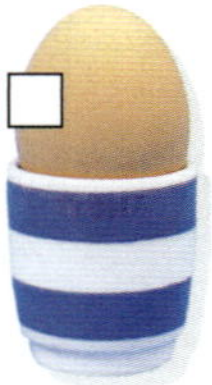
h

i

j

k

l

b 2.35 Listen and check. Then listen and repeat.

3 Work in pairs. Tell your partner:

- what food and drinks you like and don't like.
- how often you eat or drink them.
- when you eat or drink them.

PHRASE BYTES

I like / don't like …

I sometimes/never/often eat …

I eat … for breakfast / lunch / dinner / after school.

LISTEN

4 a 2.36 Read the note for Corey's family and listen. What food have they got in the house? Tick (✓) the food in Exercise 2a.

HELLO JOHNSON FAMILY. WELCOME TO ITALY! THERE'S SOME FOOD FOR YOU IN THE FRIDGE AND IN THE CUPBOARD. ENJOY YOUR HOLIDAY!

THE BERTOLINO FAMILY

b 2.36 Listen again. Match the food (a–h) to the people (1–5).

1 Corey
2 mum
3 dad
4 sister
5 brother

a chicken
b pizza
c milk
d pasta
e juice
f steak
g vegetables
h cheese

PHRASE BYTES

My favourite food is …

Rice/pasta … is popular in my country.

I like Chinese/Russian/Mexican … food.

REACT

5 Work in pairs. Ask and answer.

1 What's your favourite food?
2 What food is popular in your country?
3 Do you like food from other countries? What food?

GO BEYOND

Do the Words & Beyond exercise on page 135.

Workbook, pages 72–73

GRAMMAR *Some* and *any*, *much* and *many*

>>> Talk about how much there is of something

READ AND LISTEN >>> Grammar in context

1 2.37 **Read and listen. Which fact in Dad's book is most interesting?**

Dad: I've got some great facts about Italian food. How many courses are there in a meal? Have you got any ideas?
Corey: Three?
Dad: Four. First there are some vegetables, then there's some pasta. Then there's some meat or fish – but Italians don't eat much meat – and then something sweet. … You don't cook pasta for many minutes. How many minutes?
Mum: Ten.
Dad: No, five to six. … How much pasta does an Italian eat in a year? … More than 27 kilos!
Corey: Wow, that's a lot of pasta! How much ice cream do Italians eat?
Dad: Sorry, the book hasn't got any facts about that.

STUDY

2 Complete the table with the words in the box. Use Exercise 1 to help you.

course fish ice cream minute vegetable

Countable	Uncountable
a fact, some facts	*~~a pasta~~, some pastas*
course	*meat*
....	....

See GRAMMAR DATABASE, page 125.

3 Complete with examples from Exercise 1.

many (countable)	*much* (uncountable)
? *How many* courses *are there in a meal?*	? *How much* ...... *does an Italian eat in a year?*
✗ *You don't cook pasta for many*	✗ *Italians don't eat much* ....
✓ Positive *some* (count/uncountable)	**? ✗ Negative *any* (count/uncountable)**
I've got some	*Have you got any* ...... ? *The book hasn't got any* ....

See GRAMMAR DATABASE, page 125.

Get it right

Use *much* and *many* in questions and negatives.
Use *a lot of* in positive sentences.

>>> Workbook, page 74

4 a 2.38 PRONOUNCE **Listen and repeat the /ʌ/ sound in *much* and *some*.**

b 2.39 **Listen and repeat these words.**

brother country does hundred love

PRACTISE

5 a After a shopping trip, the Johnson family have a lot of food. Complete the sentences with *some* or *any*.

1 There's some meat.
2 There aren't ...... bananas.
3 There's ...... milk.
4 There are ...... burgers.
5 There aren't ...... lemons.
6 There isn't ...... fruit.

b Complete the conversation.

Corey: Mum, are there (1) any apples?
Mum: No, there (2) ....
Corey: Is there (3) ...... melon?
Mum: No, there (4) ....
Corey: Is there (5) ...... juice?
Mum: Yes, there (6) ....

6 a Write questions with *much* or *many*.

1 How / eggs / there?
How many eggs are there?
2 How / cheese / there?
3 How / vegetables / there?
4 How / burgers / there?
5 How / chicken / there?
6 How / bottles of water / there?

b Work in pairs. Look at the fridge in Exercise 5. Ask and answer.

How much/many … ?
There isn't much / aren't many.
There's / There are a lot of …

SPEAK

7 a Work in pairs. Student A: look at your cupboard on page 141. Say what's in it. Student B: draw the cupboard.

b Student B: look at your freezer on page 142. Say what's in it. Student A: draw the freezer.

LANGUAGE & BEYOND

»» Try new things

SCHOOL SKILLS

SPEAK AND READ

1 Work in pairs. Read what the four students say. Match them to the correct topics in the box.

new people	different free-time activities
new food	different types of music

2 Who doesn't try new things? Why not? Choose the reason they give.

… doesn't … because
- his/her friends don't do it.
- he/she doesn't feel comfortable.
- it's easier to be with the same people.

3 Why try new things? Tick (✓) what two of the students say.

The same thing is boring. ____

What can you lose? ____

You always learn something new. ____

It's fun! ____

DO

4 Make the sentences true for you. Write *often*, *sometimes* or *never*.

1 I try different food. ____
2 I listen to different types of music. ____
3 I try different free-time activities. ____
4 I make new friends and talk to different people. ____
5 I watch different types of TV programmes and films. ____

5 Work in pairs. Read your sentences to your partner. Ask why/why not.

I never try different food. *Why not?* *Because sometimes I don't like it.*

REFLECT

6 Talk about the questions. Then read the REFLECTION POINT.

1 Do you often try new things?
2 Why don't you try new things?
3 Why is it good to try new things?

PHRASE BYTES

I often try new food …

I don't try new things because …

EXTEND

7 Work in pairs. Decide what new things you can try.

I always eat cheese sandwiches for lunch. I can try salad.

I play football. I can try basketball.

REFLECTION POINT

It's easier (but sometimes boring) to do the same things. Try new things! You can learn something new, make new friends and have more fun!

Workbook, page 77

SPEAKING How much is it?

>>> Ask how much something is

SPEAK

1 Work in pairs. What do people often buy when they're on holiday? Look at the pictures and make a list together.

People often buy holiday souvenirs like …

WATCH OR LISTEN

2 2.40 Watch or listen to the scenes. What thing in Exercise 1 does each person ask about? How much is it? Complete the conversations.

1
Rico: Hi. How much is the (1) __________ ?
Poppy: It's (2) __________ euros.
Rico: OK. Can I have some, please?

2
Tara: Hello. How much is this (3) __________ ?
Kent: It's (4) __________ euros.
Tara: Sorry, that's too much.

3
Brett: How much are these (5) __________ , please?
Becca: They're (6) __________ euros.
Brett: OK. Can I have them, please?

4
Kelly: Hi. How much are the (7) __________ ?
Zac: They're (8) __________ euro.
Kelly: Mmm. I'm not sure. Thanks.

3 a 2.41 Look at the questions in the conversations. Listen and repeat.

b Make questions.

How much is	these bags?
	that fruit salad?
	the football shirt?
How much are	those pens?
	the sunglasses?
	this ice cream?

4 a 2.40 Watch or listen to conversations 1–4 again. Who buys the thing? Who doesn't buy the thing?

Rico/Tara/Brett/Kelly buys …
… doesn't buy …

b 2.42 Listen and repeat the sentences.

PHRASEBOOK 2.43

Ask how much something is

How much is the orange juice / this T-shirt / that … ?

How much are the notebooks / these … / those … ?

Buy or not buy something

OK. Can I have some/it/them, please?

Sorry, that's too much.

I'm not sure. Thanks.

ACT

5 Work in pairs. You are in the shops in Exercise 1. Practise two conversations.
Student A: ask how much something is.
Student B: say a price.
Student A: buy or don't buy the thing.
Swap roles. Then practise two more conversations.

>>> Workbook, page 75

WRITING Back home

Write a text message

READ

1 **Look at the photo. What's this food? Where do people eat it?**

2 **Read the text message. Who's it to? What's it about?**

9.30 am

Hi Jake, we're back from holiday! It's colder here than in Alicante. It's greyer too ☹. I miss the beach and the food. There aren't many bad things about Alicante! There are some good shops and I've got some great souvenirs. I've got a present for you too. See you tomorrow at school!

3 **Read the tips in the HOW TO box. Then <u>underline</u> two sentences with *too* in the text message.**

HOW TO

use *too*

- Use *too* to add another similar idea.
- Use *too* at the end of a sentence.

PRACTISE

4 **Add a similar idea. Use *too*.**

1 I like vegetables.
I like vegetables. I like fruit too.
2 I often listen to music.
3 I've got a cat.
4 There are two bedrooms in our flat.
5 I get up late on Saturdays.
6 I can speak English.

PLAN

5 **You're back home after a holiday. You're going to write a text message to a friend. Use the *Writing plan* to help you prepare.**

WRITING PLAN

1 **Say you're back. Compare your home to your holiday place.**
Is it more interesting / more boring / colder / hotter … ?

2 **Say what you miss (or don't miss).**
Do you miss the place / the people / the food / the shops?
What (good) things are there in the holiday place?

3 **Use *too* to add similar ideas.**
Read the tips in the HOW TO box.

WRITE AND CHECK

6 **Write your text message. Then check it. Tick (✓) things in the plan.**

SHARE

7 **Swap your text message with another student. Write a short answer to his/her message.**

Workbook, pages 76–77

VOCABULARY Homes

1 Complete the website post with the words in the box.

apartment balcony bathroom bedrooms dining room flat garden hall house kitchen living room swimming pool

myholidayplace.net

Tell us about your holiday places and activities!

Luis, USA

Our holiday home in Mexico isn't a small (1) ________ – or a (2) ________ as the British say – it's a big (3) ________ . It's got a (4) ________ outside with a lot of trees and a big, blue (5) ________ in it. There's also a big (6) ________ on the side of the house. Mum and Dad often sit there. There's a small (7) ________ when you come in. There are three (8) ________ to sleep in. Each one has got a (9) ________ . There's a big (10) ________ and a (11) ________ next to it to cook and eat meals and a (12) ________ with a big TV. I want to stay here!

___ /12

Food and drink

2 Complete the words.

Robbie, UK

Spain is a great holiday place. The food at the hotel is fantastic! They have all my favourite things:

- (1) br __ __ d (you eat it with (2) o __ __)
- (3) ch __ __ __ e
- (4) ch __ __ __ en
- (5) e __ __ s
- lots of fish but not much (6) m __ __ t like (7) s __ __ __ k
- orange (8) j __ __ ce
- (9) r __ __ e (mmm, paella!)
- (10) lots of ve __ __ __ __ __ __ __ es

(But there isn't much (11) p __ __ __ a and you can't get tea with (12) m __ __ k.)

___ /12

GRAMMAR Comparative adjectives

3 Complete the opinions with comparative adjectives.

What do you think?

1. Holidays are ________ (easy) than homework!
2. Swimming is ________ (nice) than school!
3. Holiday shopping with my mum is ________ (boring) than lessons!
4. T-shirts are ________ (comfortable) than my school uniform.
5. Hotel food is ________ (good) than school lunch.
6. I like school! For me, school is ________ (interesting) than the beach!

___ /12

Some and *any*, *much* and *many*

4 Choose the correct options to complete the questions and answers.

Holiday Q & A

Q How (1) ***much / many*** water do you need to drink when it's very warm?

A A lot! Always carry (2) ***some / any*** water with you.

Q How (3) ***much / many*** money do I need for a trip to Morocco? (three days)

A Morocco isn't expensive – you don't need (4) ***much / many*** money.

Q I don't like rice. How (5) ***much / many*** rice do people eat in Italy?

A You don't need to eat (6) ***some / any*** rice. There aren't (7) ***much / many*** things with rice.

___ /14

Your score: ___ /50

SKILLS CHECK

✓✓✓ Yes, I can. No problem!
✓✓ Yes, I can. But I need a bit of help.
✓ Yes, I can. But I need a lot of help.

I can read chat messages. ________
I can understand a conversation about food. ________
I can try new things. ________
I can ask how much something is. ________
I can write a text message. ________

Workbook, pages 78–79

READ

1 Match the sentences (1–5) to the correct signs (A–H).

Example:

0 Fruit isn't expensive here. *D*

1 You can buy this flat. ......

2 Small kids can't swim here. ......

3 You can have breakfast, lunch and dinner here. ......

4 You can get help in the hotel here. ......

5 You can eat this for school lunch. ......

EXAM TIPS

match sentences to signs

- Look at the example.
- Read each sentence first.
- Look for the sign with the same information.
  - Don't always look for the same words.
  - Look for different ways to say the same thing.
- You only need to use five of the signs.

A

B

C

D

E

F

G

H

Reading: ______ /10

LISTEN

2 2.44 **Listen to Matt talking to Emma about his mum and dad's jobs. For each question, choose the correct answer (A, B or C).**

Example:

0 What does Matt's mum do?
A She's a doctor.
(B) She's an actor.
C She's a cook.

1 When does Matt watch his mum?
A sometimes
B often
C never

2 Matt's dad has got a …
A shop.
B restaurant.
C café.

3 Matt's dad works from …
A 7am to 7pm.
B 7am to 10pm.
C 7am to 11pm.

4 Matt's dad's job is …
A fantastic.
B hard.
C exciting.

5 Matt's mum …
A works every evening.
B works nearly every evening.
C doesn't work every evening.

Listening: ______ /10

EXAM TIPS

listen and answer multiple-choice questions

- Read the instructions before you listen.
- Read the questions and choices.
  - What information do you need?
  - Underline the important words in the questions.
- Listen. Decide which choice is correct.
- When you listen again, check your answers.

WRITE

3 Read Jordan's invitation and message to Sam. Then complete Sam's notes.

Jordan's Picnic

Come to my big birthday picnic in City Park – Sunday 11th at 12.00.
We've got lots of food and after the picnic we can play some games too.
Hope you can come – call me by Friday (87341936).

Sam, thanks for the offer to come earlier and help with everything. We can make the food at home but we need some help at the park before the picnic. Can you come at quarter past 11? Bring your football and don't forget to wear your new football shirt too! ☺ ☺

Jordan's picnic
Why? *birthday*
Place: (1) ______
Day and date: (2) ______
Come at: (3) ______
Take: (4) ______
Remember: your (5) ______

Writing: ______ / 10

Progress check score ______ /30

EXAM TIPS

transfer information to a different text

- Read the two texts first. What are they about?
- Now read the task. What information do you need?
- Look for the information in the texts.
- Don't write sentences. Write notes.

use *and* and *but*
See page 62

use *too*
See page 72

UNIT 7

THEATRE WORKSHOP

IN THE PICTURE What are you wearing?

>>> Talk about clothes

WORK WITH WORDS Clothes

1 a RECALL **Work in pairs. Write the names of the colours. You have one minute.**

1 *red*

1	2	3	4	5	6	7	8	9	10

b Complete the clothes and accessories. What colour are they in the photos?

1 j ___ ___ ___ s ________
2 T-s ___ ___ ___ t ________
3 b ___ g ________
4 s ___ ___ g ___ ___ ___ ___ ___ s ________

2 2.45 **Listen to the descriptions. Match them to the photos.**

3 a Match the clothes (1–10) in the photos to the words in the box.

___ dress ___ hat ___ jacket ___ shirt ___ shoes ___ skirt
___ socks ___ sweatshirt ___ trainers ___ trousers

b 2.46 **Listen and check. Then listen and repeat.**

4 a 2.47 PRONOUNCE **Listen and repeat the /t/ sound in these words.**

hat shirt skirt

b 2.48 **In Exercise 3a underline four more words with the /t/ sound at the beginning, middle or end. Then listen and repeat.**

5 2.49 **Look at the photos again. Complete the sentences with words from Exercise 3a. Then listen and check.**

1 So you're wearing blue ________ , white ________ and a red ________ .
2 I like the big ________ . Very nice.
3 I'm wearing a green ________ and a brown T-shirt.
4 We've got a black ________ and a pink ________ . Are those orange ________ ? Let's see. Wow!
5 Yeah. It looks good – the yellow bag with the purple ________ and the brown ________ is good. I like it.

6 THE MOVING PICTURE **Watch the video. What are the drama group students wearing? Describe their clothes.**

a

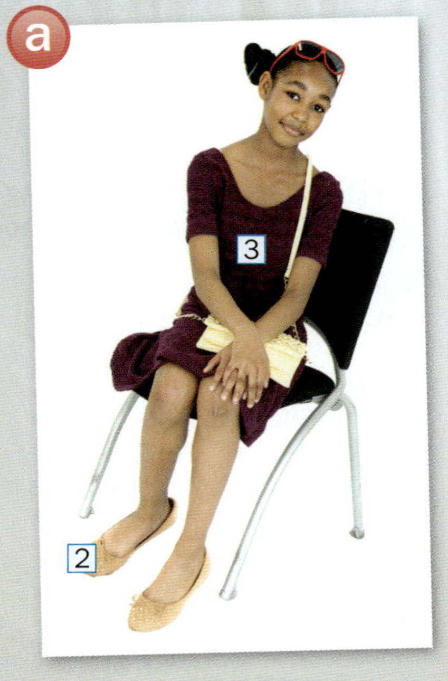

b

d

SPEAK

7 Work in pairs. Ask and answer the questions.

1 What clothes do you usually wear at school?
2 What do you wear at home?
3 What do you wear when you go out?

I usually wear …

At school/home I wear …

When I go out, I …

GO BEYOND

Do the Words & Beyond exercise on page 136.

Workbook, page 80

READING A message for the king

»» Read part of a play

SPEAK AND READ

1 Work in pairs. Ask and answer the questions.

1 How often do you go to the theatre or cinema?
2 Who are your favourite actors?
3 Are you a good actor?

READING TIP

You don't need to understand every word. Use the words that you know to help you.

2 Read the play and write the names of the people in the pictures.

a Queen

a

SCENE ONE:

The hall of King Harold's castle. There's a table in the hall with two chairs. GUARD 1 is sitting on one of the chairs. GUARD 2 is drinking some water. ALEX runs into the hall. Alex is wearing a hat, a jacket and trousers. GUARD 1 stands up.

Guard 1: Who's there?
Alex: A friend! Where are the King and Queen?
Guard 2: They're eating. What do you want, boy?
Alex: I've got a message – some important news. The Black Prince is coming.
Guard 1: I don't believe you. Stop him!

The GUARDS stop Alex.

Alex: Let me go!

The KING and QUEEN walk into the hall.

King: What's happening here?
Guard 1: It's this boy, Sir.
Alex: I'm not a boy. I'm a girl!
Guard 2: You're wearing a boy's clothes.
King: Speak, boy … girl! Why are you here?
Alex: It's the Black Prince. He's bringing 100 men here.
King: What are you saying?
Queen: She's saying the Black Prince – our son – wants to be king.
King: Where are they now?
Alex: At the moment they're sleeping in tents on the other side of the town.
Queen: Then we've got a problem!

b

c

d

e

3 Read the descriptions and write the words from the play.

1 Kings and queens often live here. .... (6 letters)
2 This person keeps other people safe. .... (5 letters)
3 Information that you give or send to someone. .... (7 letters)
4 The son of a king and queen. .... (6 letters)
5 Another way to say 'now'. .... (3 words, 2, 3, 6 letters)
6 A difficult situation. .... (7 letters)

4 2.50 Complete the tasks.

1 Form a group with four other students.
2 Each student chooses a different person from the play.
3 Listen to the play. Then read the play. Each student says their person's lines.

PHRASE BYTES

The Black Prince wants to …
Alex wears … because …
I think the King asks the guards to …

REACT

5 Work in pairs. What do you think? Tell your partner.

1 What does the Black Prince want to do?
2 What clothes does Alex wear? Why?
3 What happens next?

GO BEYOND

Write the next lines of the play.

»» Workbook, page 81

GRAMMAR Present continuous

»» Talk about things happening now

READ »» Grammar in context

1 Read Bella's text message. What's Veronique wearing?

Hello from Cardiff, the capital of Wales. I'm sending you a photo of my classmates. We aren't studying today. We're having a day off. At the moment we're walking and shopping in the city centre. (I'm not shopping because I haven't got any money!) That's Claude with Eric. He's wearing the sweatshirt with the blue stripes. He usually wears sunglasses but he isn't wearing sunglasses now. Veronique's standing next to him. She's wearing white trousers.

STUDY

2 Complete the table with examples from Exercise 1.

Present continuous
✓ Positive *I'm sending* .... *you a photo.* *He* .... *the sweatshirt.* *We're walking and* ....
✗ Negative *I'm not shopping* . *He isn't wearing sunglasses now.* *We* .... *today.*
Spelling send > *sending* have > .... shop > *shopping*
Time expressions *now* .... today

See GRAMMAR DATABASE, page 126.

PRACTISE

3 Write the *-ing* form of the verbs.

1 take *taking*
2 read ....
3 ride ....
4 play ....
5 sit ....
6 sleep ....

4 Write sentences in the present continuous.

1 I / wear / a pink shirt.
I'm wearing a pink shirt.
2 We / watch / a video.
....
3 Our teacher / write / on the board.
....
4 Students / sing / in the next room.
....
5 My best friend / swim.
....
6 My mum and dad / drive / to work.
....

5 Make the sentences in Exercise 4 true for you. Use the present continuous positive and negative.

At the moment …
1 *I'm not wearing a pink shirt. I'm wearing a white shirt.*

6 Complete the message with the present continuous.

Hello again from Wales! We (1) *'re having* (have) a fantastic time. I (2) .... (write) this postcard on the bus. We (3) .... (drive) to Caerphilly Castle. The other students (4) .... (sing). Veronique (5) .... (sit) beside me. She (6) .... (listen) to music.

SPEAK

7 Work in pairs. Student A: look at page 141. Student B: look at page 142.

- Describe your picture to your partner.
- Find six differences. Don't look at your partner's picture.

In my picture there's a girl. She's wearing a red skirt.

In my picture she's wearing a blue skirt.

LISTENING AND VOCABULARY Mime show

>>> Listen to descriptions

SPEAK AND LISTEN

1 **Work in pairs. Choose an action and mime it (act it with no words). Can your partner guess the action?**

eat listen read phone sleep

2 2.51 **Listen and match the conversations to the photos.**

1 ____ 2 ____ 3 ____ 4 ____ 5 ____

a
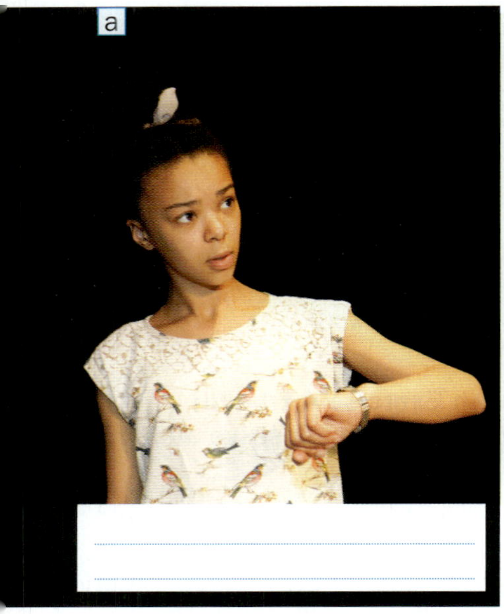

b

c

d

e
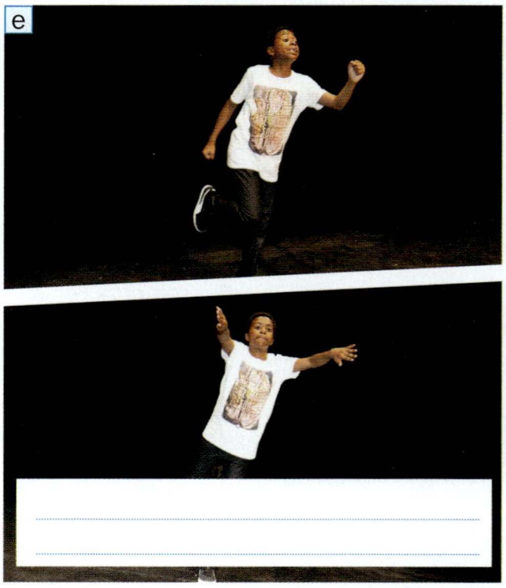

3 2.52 **Listen and check your answers.**

WORK WITH WORDS Action verbs

4 **a** **Write the action verbs under the correct photo.**

carry chat dance drive fly point
run shop sit stand swim wait

b 2.53 **Listen and check. Then listen and repeat.**

5 **a** **Complete the sentences about the mime show with the verbs in Exercise 4a. Use the present continuous.**

1 She*'s standing* on the street. She ________ for someone.
2 He ________ a bag. He ________ at something. He ________ .
3 They ________ in a car. She ________ and he ________ on the phone.
4 He ________ . No, he isn't. He ________ !
5 He ________ from someone. Now he ________ .

b 2.54 **Listen and check.**

REACT

6 **Work in pairs. Complete the tasks.**

1 Describe the mime scene you like best. Can your partner point to the correct photo?
2 Choose an action verb from Exercise 4a. Mime a new scene using the verb. Can your partner say what's happening?

You're sitting at a table.

You're eating.

GO BEYOND

Do the Words & Beyond exercise on page 136.

Workbook, pages 84–85

GRAMMAR Present continuous

»» Ask and answer questions about things happening now

READ AND LISTEN »» Grammar in context

1 2.55 **Read and listen to the conversation. When's Sally's party?**

Patrick: Hi Sally. What's happening?
Sally: Nothing.
Patrick: Oh. Where are the others? Are they waiting in the living room?
Sally: No, they aren't. Jake and Tariq are shopping.
Patrick: Is Mel making a cake?
Sally: No, she isn't.
Patrick: Oh.
Sally: What are you doing here? Why are you wearing a shirt and jacket?
Patrick: You're having a party today. Remember? Are you having a party today, Sally?
Sally: No, I'm not. The party's *next* Saturday. Patrick? Where are you going?

STUDY

2 Complete the table with examples from Exercise 1.

Present continuous
? Questions *What* are you doing *here?* *Why* ________ *a shirt and jacket?* *Where are you going?*
Are you having *a party?* ________ *a cake?* *Are they waiting in the living room?*
Short answers *Yes, I am. /* No, I'm not. *Yes, she is. /* ________ *Yes, they are. /* ________

See GRAMMAR DATABASE, page 126.

PRACTISE

3 Complete the sentences with the correct form of *be*.

1 Hi Patrick. What ___are___ you doing?
2 ________ I calling the right number?
3 ________ Patrick sleeping?
4 What ________ he doing?
5 ________ they shopping in the centre?
6 Why ________ you using Patrick's phone?

4 a Match the answers to the questions in Exercise 3.

a He's shopping with some friends. ____
b Because I'm chatting to you. ____
c No, he isn't. ____
d I'm not Patrick. I'm his brother. ___1___
e Yes, they are. ____
f Yes, you are. ____

b 2.56 **Listen and check your answers to exercises 3 and 4a.**

5 Write questions in the present continuous.

1 What / the teacher / do / at the moment?
What's the teacher doing at the moment?
2 Who / sit / next to you?
____
3 you / feel / happy at the moment?
____
4 What / the teacher / wear / today?
____
5 we / study / the present simple / now?
____
6 What / you / think / about?
____

SPEAK

6 Work in pairs. Ask and answer the questions in Exercise 5.

What's the teacher doing at the moment?

She's/He's talking to …

»» Workbook, page 86

LANGUAGE & BEYOND

>>> Be polite

SPEAK AND READ

1 **Work in pairs. Ask and answer the questions.**

1 Where can you see the signs in the photos?
2 What do they mean?
3 Do you see any signs like these on your way to school? Which ones?

2 **Write the polite words from the signs.**

please, …

PHRASE BYTES

You can see this sign on/in a …
This sign means you can't …
Yes, I do. / No, I don't.
I see a sign like this. It says …

DO

3 **Complete the sentences with the polite phrases.**

please *I'm sorry* *thank you* *excuse me*

1 ______ I'm late.
2 ______ . Can I ask a question?
3 ______ for your help.
4 Can I borrow your pen, ______ ?

4 **Work in groups. Read the situations. What do you do to be polite?**

1 You're opening a door. Someone's walking behind you.
2 You're sitting on the bus to school. An old person's getting on the bus.
3 You're reading in the school library. Your phone starts ringing.
4 You're walking home. A blind person's standing at the side of the street.

PHRASE BYTES

You wait for the person.
You ask if the person wants to …
You ask if the person needs …
You go / don't talk …
You help the person to …

REFLECT

5 **Talk about the questions. Then read the REFLECTION POINT.**

1 Which of the things in Exercise 4 do you usually do?
2 When's it important to use polite words and phrases?
3 Why do you need to look around you on a bus or train?

REFLECTION POINT

It's important to be polite when you speak and ask for things. Always think of other people and help them.

EXTEND

6 **Work in groups. Complete the tasks.**

- Choose a place: a cinema, a bus, a park, … .
- Think of a situation: Someone needs help. Some people are polite. Others aren't polite.
- Mime the scene for the other students. Can they describe what's happening?

Workbook, page 89

SPEAKING I love acting

Talk about things you like

SPEAK

1 Work in pairs. Describe the photos.

PHRASE BYTES

Kelly's carrying …
Brett's listening …
Jiya's wearing …

WATCH OR LISTEN

2 2.57 **Watch or listen to the scenes. Who loves acting?**

1 **Zac:** Hi Kelly. Where are you going?
Kelly: I'm going to my dance class. Do you want to come?
Zac: No, thanks. I (1) ______________ .
Kelly: Really? I (2) ______________ .

2 **Kelly:** Hi guys. What's wrong?
Felix: Brett (3) ______________ for the play.
Brett: I'm sorry. But it's hip hop. I (4) ______________ .
Kelly: Do you like listening to other types of music?
Brett: I (5) ______________ . Have you got any salsa? Please?

3 **Kelly:** Hey Jiya. What are you wearing?
Jiya: It's a dress for the queen. Do you like it?
Kelly: I (6) ______________ .
Jiya: I (7) ______________ . You can wear all these amazing clothes.
Kelly: I know. Excuse me. I'm late for my class.

3 a Circle the correct option.

1 Zac *likes* / *doesn't like* dancing.
2 Kelly *loves* / *hates* dancing.
3 Brett *likes* / *doesn't like* the music.
4 Brett *loves* / *hates* hip hop.
5 Brett *likes* / *doesn't like* listening to salsa.
6 Kelly really *likes* / *doesn't like* the colours.

b 2.58 **Listen and check your answers to Exercise 3a. Then listen and repeat.**

4 2.57 **Complete the conversations in Exercise 2. Use your answers to exercises 2 and 3a to help you. Watch or listen again to check your answers.**

5 a Add two things to the list. Then answer for you.

		You	Partner
Do you like …	dancing?		
	classical music?		
	acting?		
	football?		

✓✓ I love it.
✓ I like it.
✗ I don't like it.
✗✗ I hate it.

b **Work in pairs. Ask and answer the questions in Exercise 5a. Complete the table with your partner's answers.**

Do you like … ?
Yes, I do. I love it.
No, I don't.

Get it right

I love/like / don't like / hate music.
I love/like / don't like / hate listen**ing** to music.

PHRASEBOOK 2.59

Say you like something

I like music.
I like listening to music.
I love acting/dancing.
I really like …

Say you don't like something

I don't like dancing.
I hate hip hop.

Questions

Do you like it?
Do you like listening to other types of music?

ACT

6 Work in pairs. Complete the tasks.

- You meet a friend at the end of the school day.
- Write a short conversation. Start with the question: *Hi. Where are you going?*
- Use the conversations in Exercise 2 to help you.
- Present your scene to other students in the class.

Workbook, page 87

WRITING A day in the city

>>> Write a short message

READ

1 **Look at the picture. What's Jen doing?**

2 **Read the short messages. Where's Jen in each message?**

I'm sitting on the train with Tara. We're going to Manhattan. I love the city. I like walking in the park. I also love watching people.
55 minutes

Tara's shopping. She's got a new dress. She's also got some new shoes. I'm waiting for her in a café. I'm also waiting for my cola!
2 minutes

Get it right

I'm waiting ***in*** a café.

I'm waiting ***for*** her / my cola.

3 **Read the tips in the HOW TO box. Then underline three sentences with *also* in Jen's message. Circle the similar idea in the sentence before.**

HOW TO

use *also*

- Use *also* to add another similar idea.
- Use *also* after *be* and *have* with *have got*.
  She's also got some new shoes.
  I'm also waiting for my cola!
- Use *also* before other verbs.
  I also love watching people.

PRACTISE

4 **Rewrite the second sentence using *also*.**

1 I like salsa music. (I like classical music.)
I also like classical music.

2 I've got a blue jacket. (I've got a blue shirt.)

3 My dad's an actor. (He's a teacher.)

4 I go to dance classes. (I'm studying the violin.)

5 There are two cinemas in my town. (There are two theatres.)

6 We speak Spanish. (We speak some French.)

PLAN

5 **You're going to write two short messages. Use the *Writing plan* to help you prepare.**

WRITING PLAN

1 **Say where you are.**
Where are you in each message? What are you doing? Who are you with?

2 **Say what you think.**
What do you *love*, *like* or *hate*?

3 **Use *also* to add similar ideas.**
Read the tips in the HOW TO box.

WRITE AND CHECK

6 **Write your short messages. Then check them. Tick (✓) the things in the plan.**

SHARE

7 **Swap your short messages with another student. Write an answer to one of their messages.**

Workbook, pages 88–89

VOCABULARY Clothes

What can I wear tonight? 2 minutes ago

1 Write the names of the clothes.

1 .... 6 ....
2 .... 7 ....
3 .... 8 ....
4 .... 9 ....
5 .... 10 ....

___ /10

Action verbs

2 Complete the sentences with the verbs in the box.

carry chat dance drive fly point
run shop sit stand swim wait

1 .... for the cook to come.
2 .... at things I want to eat on the menu.
3 .... with Mum on the phone.
4 .... around the garden for exercise.
5 .... my new car.
6 .... for new clothes.
7 .... my shopping home.
8 .... to New York in my private plane.
9 .... in a cinema to watch my new film.
10 .... in the street for photos.
11 .... to salsa music.
12 .... in my amazing pool.

___ /12

GRAMMAR Present continuous

3 Write the verbs in the present continuous.

1 I .... (**drive**) to the cinema.
2 Lots of people .... (**stand**) on the street.
3 They .... (**wait**) to see me.
4 Now I .... (**talk**) to Ronnie Dipp, the famous actor.
5 He .... (**make**) a new film at the moment.
6 We .... (**sit**) in the cinema.
7 We .... (**have**) a fantastic time.

___ /14

Present continuous

4 Complete the questions and short answers with the present continuous.

What (1) .... now? (**you** / **do**)
I'm flying a plane.
Where (2) .... ? (**you** / **go**)
I'm going to London.
(3) .... alone? (**you** / **fly**)
(4) No, I .... I'm flying with Ronnie.
(5) .... with you now? (**he** / **sit**)
(6) Yes, he ....
Are you having lunch?
(7) No, we ....

___ /14

Your score: ___ /50

SKILLS CHECK

✓✓✓ Yes, I can. No problem!
✓✓ Yes, I can. But I need a bit of help.
✓ Yes, I can. But I need a lot of help.

I can read part of a play. ....
I can listen to descriptions. ....
I can be polite. ....
I can talk about things I like. ....
I can write a short message. ....

Workbook, pages 90–91

UNIT 8

WEATHER REPORT

IN THE PICTURE World weather

>>> Talk about the weather

Washington, the USA

Buenos Aires, Argentina

WORK WITH WORDS The weather

1 RECALL **Work in pairs. Write the countries next to the correct continent. Use the map to help you. You have two minutes. (NOTE: Two countries are in two continents.)**

~~Australia~~ Brazil Chile Germany Italy Japan
Mexico Russia South Africa the USA Turkey

AFRICA	
ASIA	
AUSTRALIA	*Australia*
EUROPE	
NORTH AMERICA	
SOUTH AMERICA	

2 a 3.01 **Match the words to the weather icons. Then listen and check.**

cloudy ___ foggy ___ raining ___
snowing ___ sunny ___ windy ___

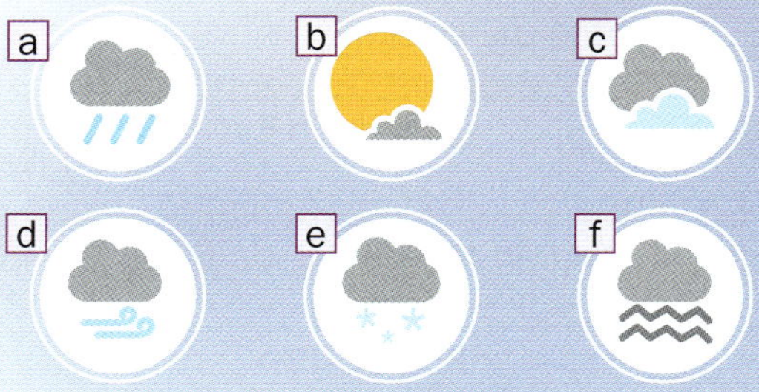

b 3.02 **Match the temperatures to the adjectives. Then listen and check.**

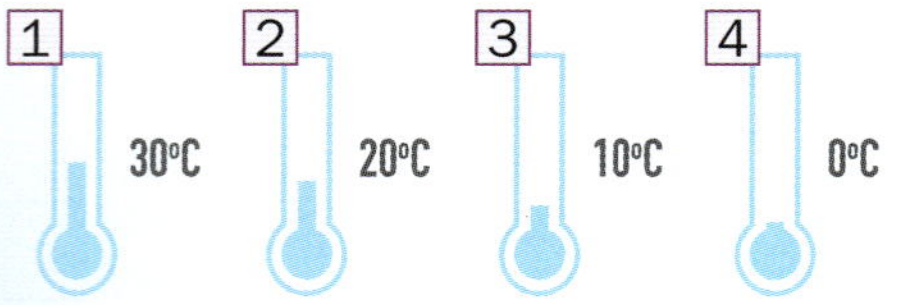

cold ___
cool ___
hot ___
warm ___

3 a Work in pairs. Match words from Exercise 2 to the five places on the world map.

b 3.03 **Listen and check or complete your answers. Then listen and repeat the weather words.**

c Choose the correct options to complete the sentences.

1 When it's hot and sunny, it's usually a *wet* / *dry* day.
2 When it's raining or snowing, it's a *wet* / *dry* day.

Moscow, Russia

Tokyo, Japan

Cape Town, South Africa

4 a 3.04 PRONOUNCE **Listen and repeat the /w/ sound in *weather*.**

b 3.05 **Listen and repeat these words.**

warm wet windy snowing world what work with words

5 THE MOVING PICTURE **Watch the video. What's the weather like in each clip?**

SPEAK

6 a Think about your answers to these questions.

1 What's the weather like today? Is it normal for this time of the year?
2 What's your favourite weather? What weather don't you like?
3 Look at the seasons in the box. Which do you have where you live? What months are they?

summer autumn winter spring
dry season rainy season

b Work in pairs. Compare your answers to Exercise 6a.

PHRASE BYTES

Today it's …

That's normal for this month/season.

It's usually … at this time of the year.

I like/love … weather.

I don't like/hate it when it's …

GO BEYOND

Do the Words & Beyond exercise on page 137.

Workbook, page 92

READING Memory

››› Read and do a test

SPEAK AND READ

1 a Look at the cartoon. Who or what has the best memory?

b Work in pairs. Can you remember the things in the box?

new English words	people's birthdays	phone numbers
phone numbers	my first teacher	my homework
my last holiday		

PHRASE BYTES

I can usually/never remember …

I sometimes forget …

I can't remember …

2 3.06 **Do the MEMORY TEST.**

3 Now read the explanation for your answers.

MEMORY TEST

HOW GOOD IS YOUR MEMORY? TAKE THIS TEST!

1 Look at this number for five seconds. Close your book. Write it.
5 3 9 1 6 2 4

2 Look at these letters for five seconds. Close your book. Write them.
G K L O F X R

3 Where were you at 6pm yesterday?

4 Who was <u>not</u> in your last class?

5 What was the weather like on Saturday morning?

6 What colour was your first school bag?

7 What were the answers to questions 1 and 2? (Don't look!)

EXPLANATION

We have *two* types of memory.
One type is just for now. It's our 'working memory'. It can remember about seven things for about 15 seconds. You use it when you put a number in your phone or do a maths problem. Questions 1 and 2 test this type of memory. Count your correct answers.

2 correct = good
1 correct = OK
0 correct = not so good

Our other memory can remember things for a long time. It's our 'long-term memory'. You use it when you remember words in English or talk to your friends about last weekend. Questions 3–7 test this type of memory. Count your correct answers.

5 correct = wow!
3–4 correct = good
2 correct = OK
0–1 correct = not so good

4 Can you remember? Answer the questions.

1 How many types of memory have we got?
2 How many things can our 'working memory' remember? For how long?

PHRASE BYTES

I think the explanation for my answers is right/wrong.

Why?

Because my working memory is/isn't …

Because I can/can't remember …

REACT

5 Work in pairs. Do you think the explanation for your answers is right or wrong? Tell your partner.

GO BEYOND

Write two more questions for the test – one for 'working memory', the other for 'long-term memory'. Give them to another student to answer.

Workbook, page 93

GRAMMAR *Was/were*

8

Describe things in the past

READ AND LISTEN Grammar in context

1 3.07 **Read and listen to the conversation. Ian and Ona were at the same place on Sunday. Where?**

Ian: Guess where I was at the weekend.
Ona: I don't know. It was a hot day. Were you at the pool?
Ian: Yes, I was – on Saturday. But I wasn't there yesterday. I was at our school.
Ona: Really? I was there too. I was in a play.
Ian: I know. I was in the audience. Was it your first play?
Ona: No, it wasn't.
Ian: Well, you were really good.
Ona: Thanks! Were Jack and Paul there?
Ian: No, they weren't. They were at the pool both days.

STUDY

2 Complete the table. Use Exercise 1 to help you.

Was/were	
Now It's a hot day.	**In the past** *It was a hot day.*
✓ Positive *I/he/she/it* was *you/we/they*	**✗ Negative** *I/he/she/it* .... *you/we/they* weren't
? Questions .... *you at the pool?* .... *it your first play?* Were *Jack and Paul there?*	**Short answers** *Yes, I was.* *No, it* wasn't *.* *No, they* .... *.*
Time expressions yesterday, at the weekend, on Saturday, last Sunday/weekend/week	

See GRAMMAR DATABASE, page 127.

PRACTISE

3 a Complete the sentences. Use *was* or *were*.

1 The weather was good. True False
2 I .... at home. True False
3 My best friends .... on the internet. True False
4 I .... happy. True False
5 My family and I .... at the cinema. True False
6 Our English teacher .... at school. True False

b Are the sentences true for you last Saturday afternoon? Circle *True* or *False*.

c Correct the false sentences. Use *wasn't* or *weren't*.

Last Saturday afternoon ...

4 Answer the questions about your first primary school. Use short answers.

1 Was it near your house?
Yes, it was. / No, it wasn't.
2 Were your best friends in your class?
3 Was it a big school?
4 Were all your teachers women?
5 Was the school cold in the winter?
6 Were you a good student?

5 Write questions about when you were six years old. Use *was* or *were*.

1 What / your first teacher's name?
What was your first teacher's name?
2 Who / your best friends?
3 your hair / long or short?
4 How old / your parents?
5 you / an only child?
6 What / your favourite food?

SPEAK

6 Work in pairs. Ask and answer the questions in Exercise 5.

Workbook, pages 94–95

LISTENING AND VOCABULARY A great day out

»» Listen to a description of a day out

WORK WITH WORDS The country

1 a Work in pairs. Match the country words in the box to the things in the photos.

beach	island	mountain	
river	sea	sky	town .....
tree	village	wood	

b 3.08 **Listen and check or complete your answers.**

2 3.09 **Listen and repeat the country words.**

3 Work in pairs. Student A: choose a word from Exercise 1a and say two words or names to describe it. Student B: say the word from Exercise 1a. Then swap roles.

Blue, cloudy.

Is it the sky?

Yes.

No. Try again.

LISTEN

4 3.10 **Isla's describing her weekend. Read the LISTENING TIP. Then listen. Which two photos above are from her weekend?**

5 3.10 **Listen again. Complete Isla's message. Write one, two or three words in the spaces.**

Hi Xenia! I'm back home again after camping in the (1) .... (I prefer the (2) .... but Mum doesn't like it.) We arrived on (3) .... evening. The weather was (4) .... on Saturday morning, but terrible in the afternoon. We went to a town. It was great – dinner in a (5) .... , a film at the cinema and I got a new (6) .... !
See you at school, Isla

REACT

6 Work in pairs. Do you prefer the beach or the mountains? Why?

LISTENING TIP

Listen first for the general idea. Don't try and understand everything.

PHRASE BYTES

I prefer … because you can …
Really? I don't like … because …

GO BEYOND

Do the Words & Beyond exercise on page 137.

Workbook, pages 96–97

GRAMMAR Past simple

>>> Talk about events in the past

READ AND LISTEN >>> Grammar in context

1 3.11 **Read and listen to the conversation. What can you see in the photo? Who isn't very happy?**

Ben: How was your day off school?
Tony: I **had** a great time. We **went** to Sky Park.
Ben: But it **rained** all day.
Tony: It **stopped** in the afternoon. There weren't many people, so we **tried** everything. We **went** on the big roller coaster too. And guess what? We **saw** Harry there. He **came** on the roller coaster with us. Look, they **took** this photo. It's so good I **bought** one for me and one for Harry.
Ben: He isn't very happy!
Tony: No. He **hated** it!

STUDY

2 Complete the examples from Exercise 1.

Past simple

✓ Positive
Regular verbs
rain > *It* rained *all day.*
hate > *He* .... *it!*
stop > *It* .... *in the afternoon.*
try > *We* .... *everything.*

See GRAMMAR DATABASE, page 127.

3 Find the past simple of the irregular verbs in Exercise 1.

1 buy	bought	4 have	....
2 come	....	5 see	....
3 go	....	6 take	....

4 3.12 PRONOUNCE **Listen and repeat the past simple verbs in exercises 2 and 3.**

>>> Workbook, page 98

PRACTISE

5 3.13 **Complete the conversation with the past simple form of the regular verbs. Then listen and check your answers.**

Tony: How was *your* day off school?
Ben: Not good.
Tony: Why?
Ben: Well, I've got exams this week so I (1) stayed (**stay**) at home in the morning and I (2) .... (**study**). I (3) .... (**chat**) with Will on the internet, but only because I (4) .... (**need**) some help. In the afternoon Lewis and I (5) .... (**play**) a game online. I (6) .... (**like**) that. But then we (7) .... (**visit**) my cousins. They're really young and it was boring. When we (8) .... (**arrive**) home, it was time for bed!

6 Write the past simple of the regular and irregular verbs. Then complete the rest of the information about your great day out.

MY GREAT DAY OUT

1 I went (**go**) to the beach (place).
2 I .... (**travel**) there by .... (transport).
3 .... (people) .... (**come**) with me.
4 The weather .... (**be**) .... (adjective).
5 We .... (**have**) .... (food) for lunch and .... (food) for dinner.
6 I .... (**take**) photos of .... (person/thing/place).
7 I .... (**see**) .... (person/thing/place).
8 I .... (**buy**) .... (souvenir/postcard/snack).

SPEAK

7 a Prepare to talk about your great day out. Practise your sentences from Exercise 6.

b Work in pairs. Tell your partner about your great day out. Try not to look at your sentences.

LANGUAGE & BEYOND

»» Be careful with money

SPEAK AND READ

1 It's the morning break at school. Lucy, Mo and Jake want to buy some food. Work in pairs and answer the questions.

(Note: 1 euro (€) = 100 cents (c))

1 How much is their food?
2 Can they buy it with their money?
3 How much is the change (= money back)?

DO

2 Work in pairs. You go to a shop. Put the money tips in the best order, from 1 to 5. Compare your answers.

.... Check your change.
.... Not enough money? Choose again.
.... Do the maths. How much do you need?
.... Look at how much money you've got.
.... Decide what you want.

3 a You're at Lucy, Mo and Jake's school. You've got €1.50 for a morning snack and €3.50 for lunch. Answer the questions.

1 What do you want for your snack and for lunch?
2 How much money do you need?
3 How much change do you get?

b Work in pairs. Tell your partner your decisions. Check your partner's maths.

PHRASE BYTES

Sandwiches are one euro seventy-five and water's …

One euro seventy-five plus (+) 60 cents is …

Three euros fifty minus (–) … is …

That's right/wrong.

REFLECT

4 Talk about the questions. Then read the REFLECTION POINT.

1 When do you need to buy things?
2 Do you always follow the tips in Exercise 2? Why?/Why not?
3 Why is it important to follow these tips?

EXTEND

5 Work in pairs. You have €10 each and want to buy a birthday present for a friend.

- Do you want to buy two smaller presents or one big one with €20?
- Think of some presents. How much do they cost? Choose what to buy.

REFLECTION POINT

It's important to be careful with money. Know how much you've got and how much you need. And always check your change.

»» Workbook, page 101

SPEAKING How are things?

8

Ask how people are

SPEAK

1 **Work in pairs. Look at the photos. How do you think the people feel – good or bad?**

WATCH OR LISTEN

2 3.14 **Watch or listen to the scenes. Check your answers to Exercise 1.**

1
Becca: Hi, Kent.
Kent: Hi, Becca. (1) ....
Becca: I'm fine. How are you?
Kent: Not too bad.

2
Felix: Hello, Rico. (2) ....
Rico: I'm fine, thanks. And you?
Felix: I'm very well, thank you.

3
Poppy: Hi, Jiya.
Jiya: Hello, Poppy. (3) ....
Poppy: Good. (4) ....
Jiya: Not too good.
Poppy: Really? Why's that?
Jiya: I don't feel very well.
Poppy: Why don't you go home?
Jiya: Yeah, good idea.

3 3.14 **Try and complete the conversations with the questions in the box. Then watch or listen again and check your answers.**

And you?	How's it going?
How are things?	How are you?

4 **Read the explanation. Then look at the conversations in Exercise 2 and answer the questions.**

BE POLITE
Use polite language when:
you don't know somebody well.
it's a formal situation.

1 In which conversation do the people use polite language? How do you know?
2 What polite questions do they use? Can you use these questions with everybody?
3 Which questions can you only use with friends?

5 3.15 **Listen and repeat the questions and answers.**

PHRASEBOOK 3.16

Ask how people are
How are you?
How are things?
How's it going?
And you?

Say how you are
Good.
Not too bad.
I'm fine (thanks).
I'm very well (thank you).
Not too good.

ACT

6 **Work in pairs. Complete the tasks.**

- Prepare two scenes at school: one scene with two friends, the other with a student and a teacher.
- In the scenes the people say *hello* and ask how the other person is.
- Practise your scenes. Then present them to other students.

Workbook, page 99

WRITING Send me a postcard

»» Write a postcard

SPEAK AND READ

1 **Work in pairs. How often do you send postcards? How often do you get them? When was the last time?**

2 **Read the postcard. (Don't worry about the mistakes!) Why wasn't yesterday a perfect day?**

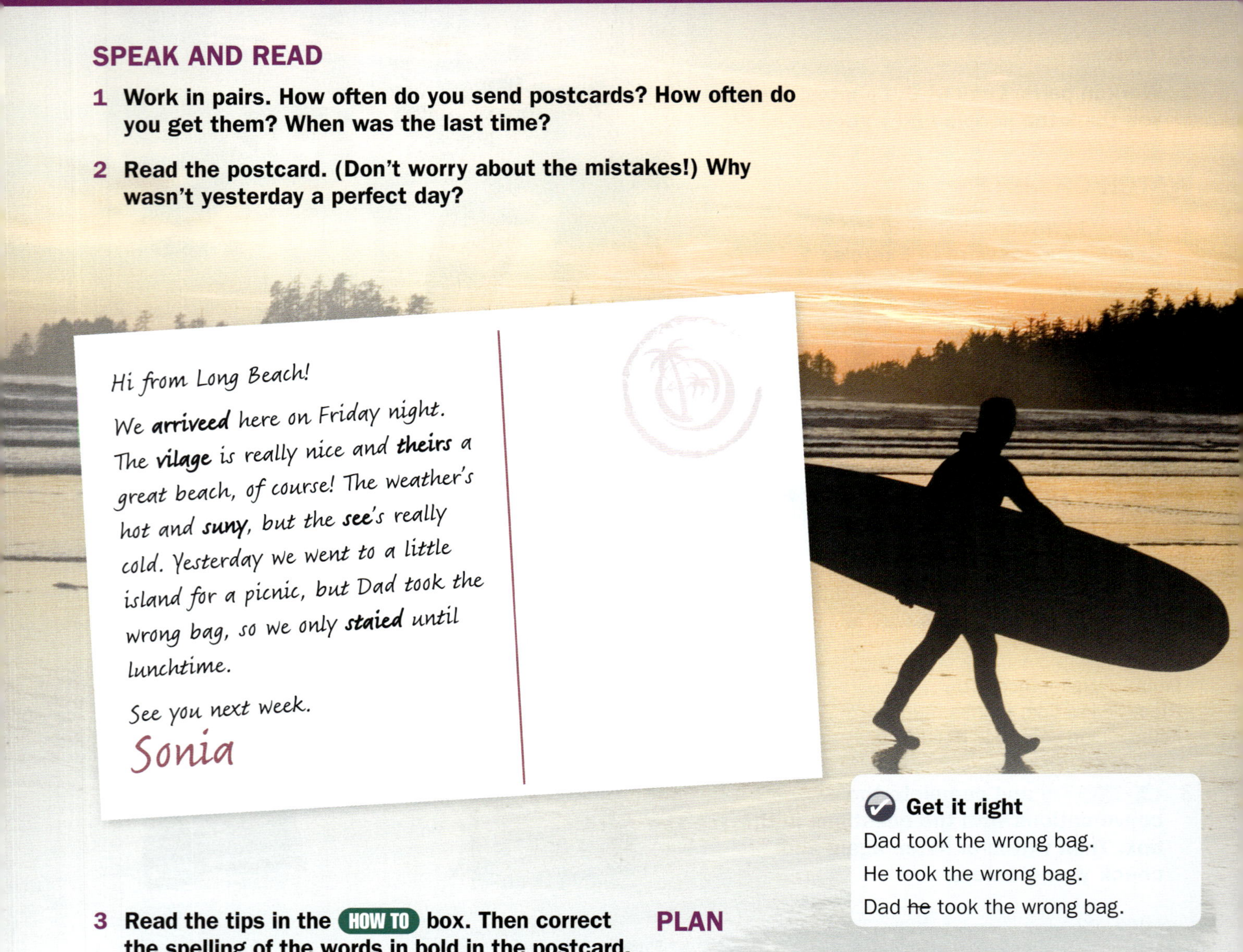

Hi from Long Beach!

We **arriveed** here on Friday night. The **vilage** is really nice and **theirs** a great beach, of course! The weather's hot and **suny**, but the **see**'s really cold. Yesterday we went to a little island for a picnic, but Dad took the wrong bag, so we only **staied** until lunchtime.

See you next week.

Sonia

Get it right

Dad took the wrong bag.

He took the wrong bag.

Dad ~~he~~ took the wrong bag.

3 **Read the tips in the HOW TO box. Then correct the spelling of the words in bold in the postcard.**

HOW TO

check your spelling

- Check for double letters: *arrive* (NOT ~~*arive*~~), *holiday* (NOT ~~*holliday*~~).
- Check verbs: *tried* (NOT ~~*tryed*~~), *enjoyed* (NOT ~~*enjoied*~~).
- Check words with the same pronunciation: *there/their*, *it's/its*.

PRACTISE

4 **Choose the correct spelling of each word.**

1 Yesterday we *visited* / *visitted* a town in the mountains.
2 We *stoped* / *stopped* for lunch on the way.
3 It was a *fogy* / *foggy* day.
4 It was very cold *too* / *two* .
5 I hope you're *having* / *haveing* better weather.
6 *Write* / *Right* soon!

PLAN

5 **You're going to write a postcard. Use the *Writing plan* to help you prepare.**

WRITING PLAN

1 **Decide where you are.**
Is it a place in your country or another country?

2 **Describe the place and weather.**
Is it a city or in the country? Is it hot or cold?

3 **Say what you did yesterday.**
Think about activities, food and your daily routine.

WRITE AND CHECK

6 **Write your postcard. Then check it. Tick (✓) the things in the plan.**

SHARE

7 **Swap your postcard with other students. Which trip sounds the most enjoyable? Why?**

»» Workbook, pages 100–101

VOCABULARY The weather

1 Complete the weather words.

WEATHER ALERTS

30°C 9am: It's (1) h ______ and (2) s ______ and a very (3) d ______ morning.

20°C 1pm: It's (4) w ______ but it's also (5) c ______ and a little (6) w ______.

3°C 5pm: It's (7) c ______ and (8) f ______ and it's (9) s ______ too.

10°C 9pm: It's (10) c ______ and it's (11) r ______. Prepare for a (12) w ______ night.

___ /12

The country

2 Match the words in the box to the things in the picture.

___ beach	___ island	___ mountain
___ river	___ sea	___ sky
___ town	___ tree	___ village
___ wood		

___ /10

GRAMMAR *Was/were*

3 Complete the TV interview with *was/wasn't* and *were/weren't*.

Presenter: I'm talking to Judy Murray about the bad weather yesterday. Judy, (1) ______ it bad when you started walking?
Judy: No, it (2) ______.
Presenter: (3) ______ you prepared for bad weather?
Judy: No, we (4) ______. And it changed very fast.
Presenter: What (5) ______ the weather like?
Judy: Terrible. We (6) ______ really frightened.
Presenter: Judy, thanks for talking to us.

___ /12

Past simple

4 Complete the news story with the past simple form of the verbs.

Judy Murray and her family (1) ______ (**start**) walking at 10am in good weather. They (2) ______ (**buy**) sandwiches in a local shop, and at 1pm they (3) ______ (**stop**) walking and they (4) ______ (**have**) lunch high up in the mountains. That's when the snow (5) ______ (**come**). At 5pm Judy (6) ______ (**phone**) the police for help. Two teams of police officers (7) ______ (**go**) to find them. It was 9pm when they finally (8) ______ (**take**) the family back home.

___ /16

Your score: ___ /50

SKILLS CHECK

✓✓✓ Yes, I can. No problem!
✓✓ Yes, I can. But I need a bit of help.
✓ Yes, I can. But I need a lot of help.

I can read and do a test. ______
I can listen to a description of a day out. ______
I can be careful with money. ______
I can ask how people are. ______
I can write a postcard. ______

Workbook, pages 102–103

READ

1 **Read the blog post about Buenos Aires. Choose the best word (A, B or C) for each space.**

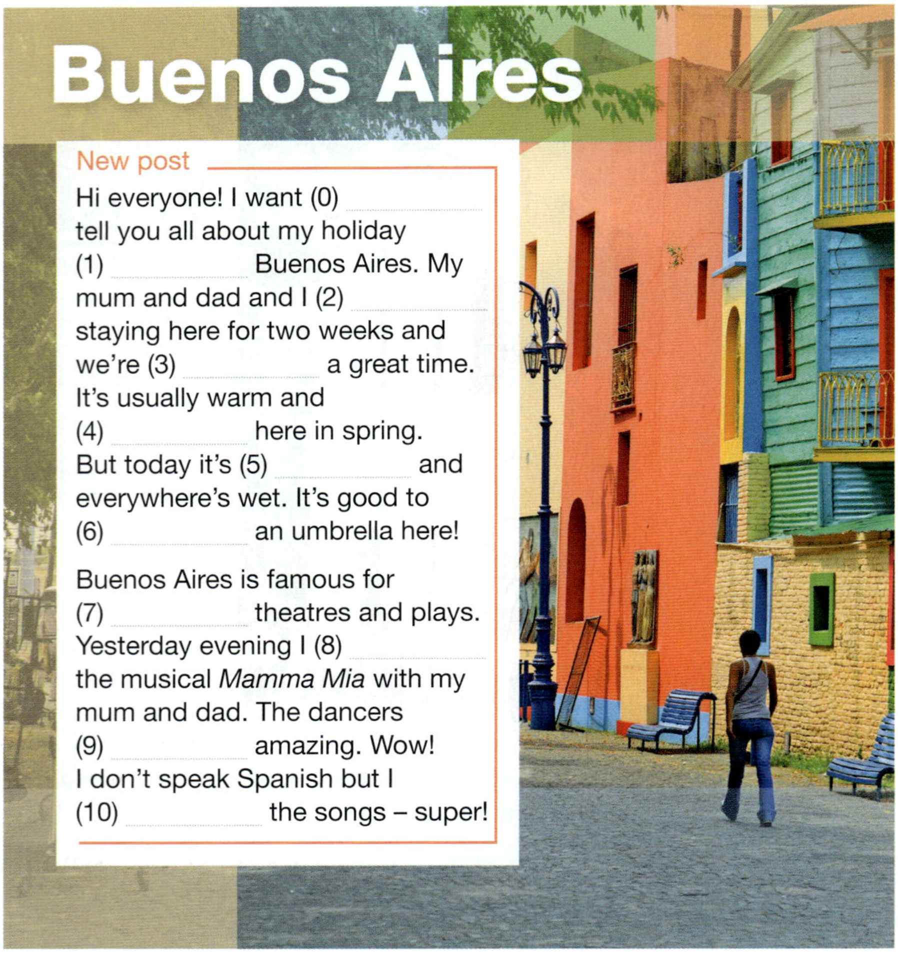

Buenos Aires

New post

Hi everyone! I want (0) .... tell you all about my holiday (1) .... Buenos Aires. My mum and dad and I (2) .... staying here for two weeks and we're (3) .... a great time. It's usually warm and (4) .... here in spring. But today it's (5) .... and everywhere's wet. It's good to (6) .... an umbrella here!

Buenos Aires is famous for (7) .... theatres and plays. Yesterday evening I (8) .... the musical *Mamma Mia* with my mum and dad. The dancers (9) .... amazing. Wow! I don't speak Spanish but I (10) .... the songs – super!

Example:

0	A not	B for	(C) to
1	A at	B in	C on
2	A am	B is	C are
3	A have	B having	C had
4	A sunny	B foggy	C windy
5	A hot	B raining	C dry
6	A point	B shop	C carry
7	A their	B his	C its
8	A saw	B went	C had
9	A was	B were	C weren't
10	A hated	B listened	C loved

Reading: ________ /10

EXAM TIPS

complete gaps in a text with multiple-choice answers

- Quickly read the text. What's it about?
- Look at the example. It shows you what to do.
- Read each sentence. Do you have an idea for the gap?
- Look at the choices. Is your idea there?
- If not, choose the best word.

LISTEN

2 3.17 **Listen to five conversations. You will hear each conversation twice. Choose the correct answer for each question (A, B or C). Then listen again.**

Example:

0 Where was Peter yesterday?

A  Ⓑ  C 

1 What's Bella's favourite music?

A  B  C 

2 What's Jacob doing?

A  B  C 

3 How old is Kira's sister?

A 

B 

C 

4 What's on the floor?

A 

B  C 

5 How much is Lucy's lunch?

A €2.00 Thank you for shopping with us!

B €2.95 Thank you for shopping with us!

C €2.05 Thank you for shopping with us!

Listening: ________ / 10

WRITE

3 Read the descriptions and complete the country words.

Example:

0 This long area of water goes to the sea. r *i* *v* *e* *r*

1 It's a very small town in the country. v _ _ _ _ _ _

2 It's very high and it often has snow on it. m _ _ _ _ _ _ _

3 It's near the sea and people often lie on it in the sun. b _ _ _ _

4 It's an area of land with water all around it. i _ _ _ _ _

5 There are lots of trees in it. w _ _ _ _

________ /5

4 Read the message from your friend Aiden. Write a reply. Tell him what you're doing (25–35 words).

> Hi, I'm bored! Are you at home? What are you doing now? Do you want to come to my house and play computer games?

________ /5

Writing: ________ / 10

Progress check score ________ /30

EXAM TIPS

answer multiple-choice questions with pictures

- Read the questions before you listen.
- Look at the pictures. What English words and numbers can you see?
- Listen for these words and numbers, and for the main ideas.
- When you listen again, check your answers.

EXAM TIPS

complete words from descriptions

- Look at the example and the other questions.
- Read the description and the first letter. Can you think of the word?
- Check the number of letters. (One line = one letter.)
- Check your spelling.

EXAM TIPS

reply to an email or message

- Read the email or message.
- Write your reply. Answer all the questions in the email or message.
- Use the correct number of words.

use *also*

See page 84

check your spelling

See page 94

Download extra speaking activities from the *Beyond* website.

UNIT 9 ONE DAY

IN THE PICTURE Dates

»» Talk about dates

WORK WITH WORDS Dates

1 a RECALL **Work in pairs. Write the correct days and months. You have one minute.**

1 Two months with an 'l'
2 Day 5 (Day 1 = Monday)
3 A month with nine letters
4 The days of the weekend
5 A month with 28 or 29 days
6 This day sounds different to the spelling.

b Work in pairs. Say all the days of the week and the months very quickly.

2 Look at Marco's calendar journal. Where was he on the first day and last day of May?

3 a 3.18 **Look at the dates. Listen and repeat.**

1st May = *the first of May*

2nd May = *the second of May*

3rd May = *the third of May*

4th May = *the fourth of May*

5th May = *the fifth of May*

WRITE	SAY
1st May	*the first of May*
OR	
May 1st	*May the first*

b 3.19 **Look at the other numbers. Listen and repeat.**

6th sixth	11th eleventh	16th sixteenth	20th twentieth
7th seventh	12th twelfth	17th seventeenth	21st twenty-first
8th eighth	13th thirteenth	18th eighteenth	30th thirtieth
9th ninth	14th fourteenth	19th nineteenth	31st thirty-first
10th tenth	15th fifteenth		

c 3.20 PRONOUNCE **Listen and repeat the /θ/ sound in these words.**

fourth fifth twelfth thirtieth

4 a Say what Marco did on these days:

6th May 12th May 16th May 28th May

On the sixth of May Marco …

b Work in pairs.
Student A: say a date. Student B: say what happened on that date. Then swap roles.

5 **THE MOVING PICTURE** **Watch the video. Complete Marco's calendar journal for the dates with no information.**

6 3.21 **Read and listen to Marco's list of special dates. Look at the box and say the dates.**

MY SPECIAL DATES

1 12th November 2008: We moved to this town.
2 1st August 2012: My family went to the USA on holiday. It was fantastic.
3 20th February 2014: I bought a bike with my birthday money.

WRITE	SAY
2000	*two thousand*
2009	*two thousand and nine*
2010	*twenty ten*

WRITE AND SPEAK

7 a **Write three special dates for you. Why were they special?**

b **Work in pairs. Tell your partner about your special dates. Your partner makes notes. Then tell the class one thing about your partner.**

Antonella had a big birthday party on the nineteenth of September 2013.

GO BEYOND

Do the Words & Beyond exercise on page 138.

Workbook, page 104

READING The wrong day

Read a book review

SPEAK AND READ

1 **Work in pairs. When was your last birthday? Tell your partner about your last birthday present(s).**

2 3.22 **Read the review of a comic book. What was Zadie's birthday present?**

PHRASE BYTES

My last birthday was on …

I got some socks / some money / a phone …

I can't remember what I got.

REVIEW BY: Lena P.
TITLE: *Zadie in Z-land*

Story:

For Zadie's birthday on 16th August 2045, her grandad gave her a very special present. It was a time machine. Zadie knew what date she wanted to visit first: 13th May 2043, a happy day in her life. On that day Zadie got her cat Zed and she met her friend Zuni for the first time.

There was just one problem. Grandad's time machine didn't work: the dates in the computer were all wrong. So Zadie didn't travel back to 13th May 2043, she travelled to 31st May 2043. And that date *wasn't* a good day in Zadie's life.

On 31st May she lost Zed and he didn't come back again. She lost her favourite ring and she didn't find it again. Her friend Zuni ate something bad and got really ill. And Zadie didn't see a glass door at computer school and walked into it. She didn't get hurt but everybody laughed. It was a terrible day.

Your opinion: ★★★★★

Fantastic! I loved this book.

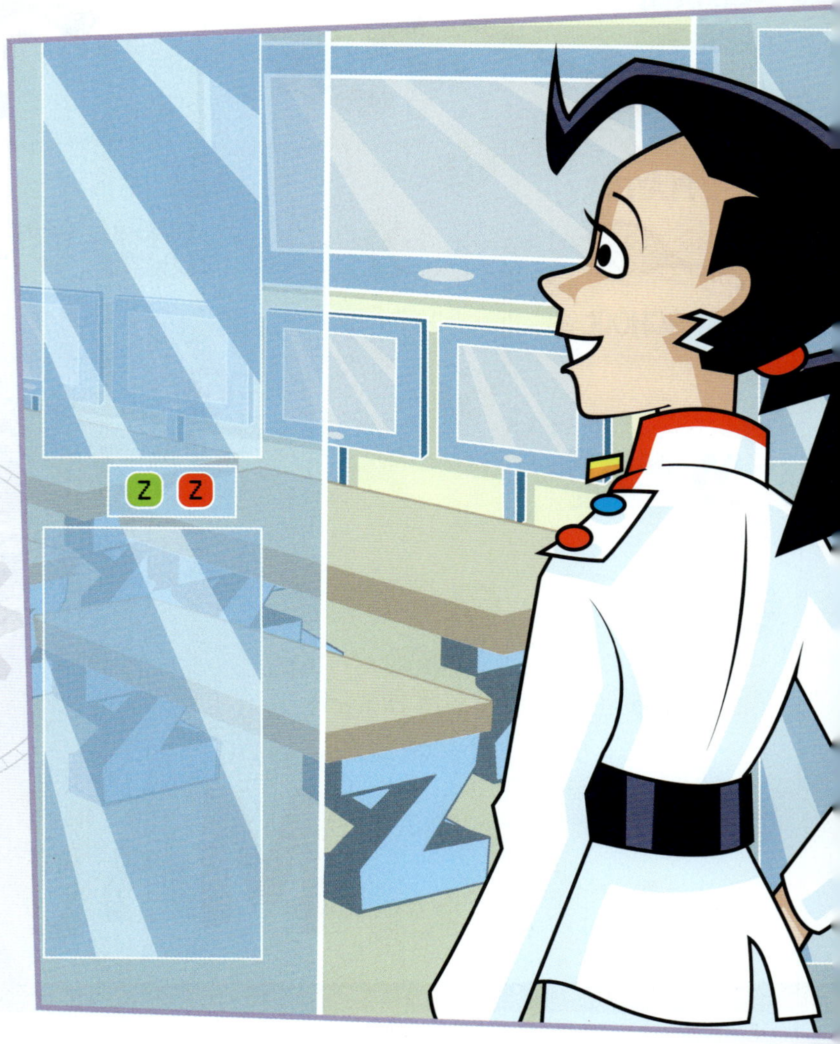

3 **Read the review again. Finish the sentences.**

1 Zadie wanted to visit … because …
2 There was a problem with the …
3 Zadie travelled to …
4 May 31st wasn't …
5 The reader loved …

4 **Match the sentence halves.**

1 Her grandad **gave** her
2 Zadie **knew**
3 Zadie **got**
4 She **met**
5 She **lost**
6 Zuni **ate**

a something bad.
b her favourite ring.
c her cat Zed.
d a special present.
e her friend Zuni.
f what date she wanted to visit.

5 **Look at the past simple verb forms in Exercise 4. Write the verbs.**

1 *gave – give*

PHRASE BYTES

I like/love/hate reading …

I think this book is/isn't interesting … because …

I choose … because …

REACT

6 **Work in pairs. What do you think? Tell your partner.**

1 Do you like reading books? Is *Zadie in Z-land* the right book for you?
2 You're in a time machine. What date do you choose? Why?

GO BEYOND

What happened to Zed the cat? Think of two or three ideas.

Workbook, page 105

GRAMMAR Past simple

9

Talk about what didn't happen in the past

READ Grammar in context

1 Read the end of the comic book. Find out where Zadie went. Was it a good place?

STUDY

2 Complete the explanation. Then write examples from Exercise 1.

Past simple

✗ Negative regular and irregular verbs
I/you/she, etc ________ + verb

Her friends didn't have *time to be with her.*
On this day she ________ *to the past.*
The future Z-land ________ *good.*
Zadie ________ *to travel again.*

See GRAMMAR DATABASE, page 128.

Get it right

Don't use the past form after *didn't*.
~~didn't had~~ didn't *have*
~~didn't wanted~~ didn't *want*

Remember: The past simple negative of *be* is *wasn't/weren't*.

PRACTISE

3 Choose the correct options to complete the sentences.

1 Zadie *had* / *didn't have* homework, so she listened to music.
2 She *ate* / *didn't eat* lunch because she wasn't hungry.
3 Later she *visited* / *didn't visit* Zuni and they watched a film.
4 The film was terrible and they *liked* / *didn't like* it.
5 Then they *knew* / *didn't know* what to do, so Zadie went home.
6 She *went* / *didn't go* to bed and dreamed of …

4 Complete the description. Use the past simple negative of the correct verb.

eat go ~~live~~ look travel wear

In Zadie's dream she (1) didn't live in 2045 – it was the year 2015.
She (2) ________ to computer school – she studied at a real school with teachers.
The students (3) ________ in flying cars – they used bikes.
They (4) ________ clothes like hers – they all had trousers and shirts.
They (5) ________ superfood for lunch – they had pizza and chips.
But they (6) ________ sad – they were happy.

5 Write sentences with the past simple negative.

I had a dream last night. In my dream …

1 I didn't have black hair and brown eyes. I had green hair and pink eyes.
2 I ________ in England. I lived in India.
3 I ________ many people. I only knew my parents.
4 I ________ to school by car. I went to school on a horse.
5 I ________ bread for breakfast. I ate rice.
6 It ________ every day. In fact, it never rained!

WRITE AND SPEAK

6 a You had a dream. Write three to five sentences about your dream. What was different about you or your life?

I didn't … I …

b Work in pairs. Tell your partner about your dream.

I had a dream last night.
Tell me about it.
Well, I didn't …

Workbook, pages 106–107

LISTENING AND VOCABULARY What did they say?

⋙ Understand short conversations

SPEAK AND LISTEN

1 Work in pairs. Write the opinion adjectives in two lists: positive ☺ and negative ☹.

boring	cool	difficult	easy	exciting	fantastic	friendly
good	happy	hard	interesting	popular	special	

LISTENING TIP

Listen for important verbs, nouns and adjectives.

2 ▶3.23 Listen to five conversations about people's days. Choose the correct answer (A, B or C).

1 What did Declan get for his birthday?

A  B  C 

2 Where did Keri and her mum go?

A 

B 

C 

3 Who did Seth's dad speak to?

A  B  C 

4 Which bag did Lea buy?

A 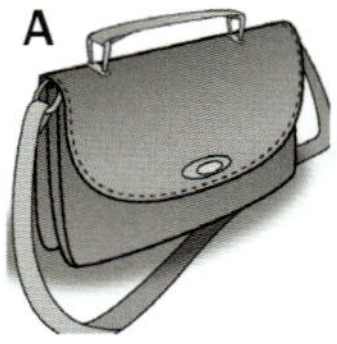 B  C 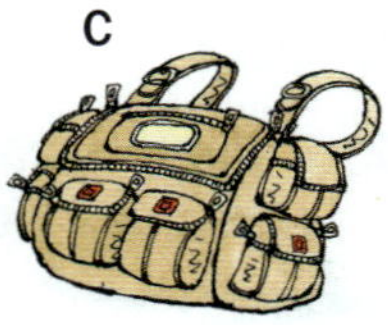

5 What was really interesting for Diego?

A 

B 

C 

3 ▶3.23 Listen again. For each thing in Exercise 2, write one of the adjectives from Exercise 1.

WORK WITH WORDS Adjectives of opinion

4 a ▶3.24 What do all the words in the box mean? Choose A, B or C. Then listen and repeat.

amazing	brilliant	excellent	lovely	wonderful

A boring **B** fantastic **C** happy

b ▶3.25 Complete the sentences with the words in the box. Then listen and check.

beautiful	important	pretty	strange	useful

1 Your dress looks nice. It's ....
2 Your dress looks very nice. It's ....
3 Don't forget that date – it's very ....
4 I've got a new phone. It can do everything! It's very ....
5 I don't understand it. It's very ....

5 a ▶3.26 PRONOUNCE Listen and repeat the long /eɪ/ sound in these words.

amazing strange

b ▶3.27 Listen and repeat these words.

day date grey place say

PHRASE BYTES

I got … as a present from … It's …

I think … is a beautiful place because …

… is very important to me because …

REACT

6 Work in pairs. Choose one thing and tell your partner about it.

- a brilliant or useful present
- a beautiful place
- something or somebody important to you

GO BEYOND

Do the Words & Beyond exercise on page 138.

⋙ Workbook, pages 108–109

GRAMMAR Past simple

»» Ask about things in the past

READ AND LISTEN »» Grammar in context

1 3.28 **Read and listen to the interview with a teacher. What was his day like?**

A DAY IN THE LIFE OF OUR TEACHERS

DANIKA: Did you have a good day?
MR EVANS: Yes, I did.
DANIKA: How many lessons did you teach?
MR EVANS: Six English lessons. Then at lunch time I had the reading club.
DANIKA: Did you have any free time?
MR EVANS: No, I didn't. It was a very busy day.
DANIKA: Did your students work hard?
MR EVANS: Yes, they did. My students always work hard.

STUDY

2 Complete the examples with words from Exercise 1.

Get it right

Remember: The past simple question form of *be* is *Was she … ? / Were you … ?*, etc.

Past simple

? Questions and short answers

.... you have a good day?
Yes, I *did* .
.... you have any free time?
No, I ....
.... your students work hard?
Yes, they ....
How many lessons .... you teach?
Six English lessons.

See GRAMMAR DATABASE, page 128.

PRACTISE

3 a Make more questions for Mr Evans. Put the words in order.

1 you / did / What time / get up?
What time did you get up?
2 come / you / to school / Did / by car?
3 get / did / you / When / to school?
4 you / something / Did / eat / for lunch?
5 did / What / your reading club students / talk about?
6 too many / I / Did / ask / questions?

b Match Mr Evans's answers to the questions.

a Yes, I did. I had a sandwich. *4*
b No, you didn't. ....
c I got to school at 8 o'clock. ....
d I got up at half past six. ....
e No, I didn't. I came by bus. ....
f They talked about a book called *Zadie in Z-land*. ....

4 a Write the questions. Use the words in brackets.

1 *Did you have* (you / have) a shower this morning?
2 .... (your mum / cook) breakfast for you?
3 .... (you / come) to school by bus?
4 .... (you / get) to school late?
5 .... (your English teacher / say) good morning?
6 .... (your English lesson / start) on time?

b Work in pairs. Ask and answer the questions in Exercise 4a.

Did you have a shower this morning?

Yes, I did.

No, I didn't. I had a shower yesterday evening.

WRITE AND SPEAK

5 a Work in groups. Write three past simple questions. They can be funny or strange.

b For each question, write each word or phrase on a big piece of paper. Give your questions to another group. Then each group stands with the question in the correct order. One student from the class answers the question.

Workbook, page 110

LANGUAGE & BEYOND

Do you know the story of ______________? His 'father' Geppetto made him from wood. He wasn't a real boy, but he walked and talked. He wasn't a nice boy or an honest boy. One day his father gave him money for a school book. But the boy didn't buy a book; he bought a ticket for a circus show. Later he lied to his father: he lost the money, he said. Another day he didn't go to school and he played games with his friend.
Every time he wasn't honest, his nose got longer.

»» Act in an honest way

READ

1 a Read the story. Do you know it? What's the name of the boy?

b When wasn't the boy honest? Find three examples.

DO

2 Work in pairs. Decide which situations (1–5) are honest (*H*) and not honest (*NH*).

3 Work in pairs. What happens when you aren't honest in the situations in Exercise 2? Choose one or two of ideas a–d for each situation.

a You feel bad because you did something wrong.
b Another student can't do something.
c People think bad things about another student.
d You don't learn anything.

Is it honest?

1 You tell a classmate something bad about another classmate. It isn't true. ......
2 You break a window at school. You tell your teacher about it. ......
3 You copy a friend's homework because you didn't do yours. ......
4 You write the answers to a test on your hand. Nobody sees you. ......
5 You find some money at school. You give it to your teacher. ......

4 Is it OK not to be 100% honest in these situations? Why?/Why not?

1 Your friend has some new clothes. They don't look good. You say they look good.
2 Your mum cooks dinner and it isn't very nice. You say you aren't hungry.

REFLECT

5 Talk about the questions. Then read the REFLECTION POINT.

1 Is it hard to be honest?
2 How do you feel when you aren't honest?
3 How do other people feel?

PHRASE BYTES

It's hard / It isn't hard ...
When you aren't honest, you feel ...
When you aren't honest, other people ...

EXTEND

6 Work in pairs. Choose one scene. Act the scene in two different ways – one time *not honest* and the other *honest*.

- You went on the internet for one hour. Your mum/dad said 30 minutes.
- You came home very late because you went out with friends. Your mum/dad isn't happy.
- You looked at a friend's journal. He/She saw you with the book.

REFLECTION POINT

Be honest when you say and do things. When you aren't honest, you feel bad. You can also hurt other people.

SCHOOL SKILLS

Workbook, pages 113

SPEAKING Yes, please

Offer something to somebody

SPEAK

1 **Look at the photos. What do you think Rico and Poppy are offering to Tara, Brett and Felix?**

WATCH OR LISTEN

2 3.29 **Watch or listen to the scenes. Check your answers from Exercise 1. Do you think Brett is honest?**

1
Rico: (1) ______________ ?
Tara: Are you sure?
Rico: Yes. I don't really like oranges.
Tara: OK then – yes, please. (2) ______________ ?
Rico: No, thanks. I don't like fruit.

2
Poppy: (3) ______________ , Brett?
Brett: What have you got?
Poppy: (4) ______________ ? Or would you like a banana sandwich?
Brett: Er, no, thanks. I'm not very hungry.
Poppy: OK. (5) ______________ , Felix?
Felix: I'd like a fish sandwich *and* a banana sandwich, please.
Poppy: Fine. … Here you are.

3 **a** **Work in pairs. Write these questions in the correct places in the conversations in Exercise 2.**

a What about you?
b What would you like?
c Would you like my apple?
d What about a fish sandwich?
e Would you like my orange?

b 3.29 **Watch or listen again and check.**

c 3.30 **Listen and repeat the questions.**

4 **Work in pairs. In the two conversations find a phrase to …**

1 say you want something ______________
2 say you don't want something ______________
3 check something ______________
4 explain what you want ______________

ACT

5 **Work in pairs. Complete the tasks.**

- **You're at school and it's lunchtime. Student A: offer your partner things from your lunchbox. Student B: look at page 142 and answer your partner.**
- **Your friend has come to your house for the first time. Student B: offer your partner different things to eat and drink. Student A: look at page 141 and answer your partner.**

PHRASEBOOK 3.31

Offer something
Would you like a(n) … /some … ?
What about … ?
What would you like?
What about you?

Reply to an offer
Are you sure?
Yes, please.
No, thanks.
I'd like a(n)/some …

Workbook, page 111

WRITING My weekend

Write chat messages about your weekend

SPEAK AND READ

1 Work in pairs. Talk about activities you usually do at the weekend.

I usually play football on Saturday.

I always ...

Get it right

at the weekend

on Saturday/Sunday

2 Read the chat messages. What did Andrei and Dario do at the weekend?

3 Read the tips in the HOW TO box. Then find two sentences with *because* in the chat messages.

HOW TO

use *because*

- Use *because* to say 'why'.
- Use *because* to link two sentences.
- Don't use *because* to start a sentence.

PRACTISE

4 Match the sentence halves.

1 It was an important day
2 I stayed in bed all day
3 We cleaned the flat
4 I watched TV
5 We went shopping
6 We didn't go out

a because there was a good film on.
b because it was very dirty.
c because the weather was terrible.
d because I needed some new jeans.
e because I was ill.
f because it was my dad's 40th birthday.

PLAN

5 You're going to write chat messages with a partner in your class. Use the *Writing plan* to help you prepare.

WRITING PLAN

1 **Write a question about your partner's weekend.**
(Use the past simple.) ☐

2 **Your partner writes an answer.**
Write about activities on Saturday and Sunday.
(Use the past simple.) ☐

3 **Your partner asks about your weekend.**
Was it a good weekend? ☐

4 **Write what you did and why it was good or bad.**
Read the tips in the HOW TO box. ☐

WRITE AND CHECK

6 Work in pairs. Write your chat messages. Then check them. Tick (✓) the things in the plan.

SHARE

7 Swap your chat messages with other students. Who did something exciting at the weekend?

Workbook, pages 112–113

VOCABULARY Dates

1 Write the dates in words.

My calendar and journal
Important dates

23.01.2012
the (1) ______ of January, (2) ______

12.10.2005
the (3) ______ of October, (4) ______

07.11.2014
the (5) ______ of November, (6) ______

02.02.2010
the (7) ______ of February, (8) ______

30.04.2009
the (9) ______ of April, (10) ______

___ /10

Adjectives of opinion

2 Complete the adjectives.

Sunday, 17th June

1 This was an im _ _ _ _ _ _ t day for Mum. It was her birthday.
2 It was a wo _ _ _ _ _ _ l day.
3 The weather was l _ _ _ _ y.
4 Her new dress was very pr _ _ _ y.
5 The food was ex _ _ _ _ _ _ t.
6 The table looked be _ _ _ _ _ _ l.
7 Her presents were br _ _ _ _ _ _ t.
8 Her new shoes were am _ _ _ _ g.
9 Her present from Grandma was very us _ _ _ l.
10 The present from Dad was very st _ _ _ _ e.

___ /10

GRAMMAR Past simple

3 Write sentences with *I* and the correct past simple form of the verbs.

This was a good weekend :)

get up / at 7.00 (✗)
(1) ______
get up / at 11.00 (✓)
(2) ______
have / breakfast at 7.30 (✗)
(3) ______
have / breakfast at 11.30 (✓)
(4) ______
do / homework (✗)
(5) ______
do / lots of fun things (✓)
(6) ______
go / to bed early (✗)
(7) ______

___ /14

Past simple

4 Write the past simple questions and answers.

How was your month?

1 you / have / a good month?
______
2 Yes, ______ .
3 your mum and dad / plan / any special days?
______
4 Yes, ______ .
5 you and your friends / do / anything new?
______
6 No, ______ .
7 anything bad / happen?
______
8 No, ______ .

___ /16

Your score: ___ /50

SKILLS CHECK

✓✓✓ Yes, I can. No problem!
✓✓ Yes, I can. But I need a bit of help.
✓ Yes, I can. But I need a lot of help.

I can read a book review. ______
I can understand short conversations. ______
I can act in an honest way. ______
I can offer something to somebody. ______
I can write chat messages about my weekend. ______

Workbook, pages 114–115

UNIT 10 SPORTS TIME

IN THE PICTURE Spot the ball

Talk about where things are

WORK WITH WORDS Prepositions of place

1 RECALL **Work in pairs. Look at the photos and complete the task. You have two minutes.**

Write the names of:

- three sports. *football, ...*
- four 'clothes' items.
- five colours.
- six parts of the body.

2 a Write the words under the pictures.

above behind between in in front of near next to on opposite under

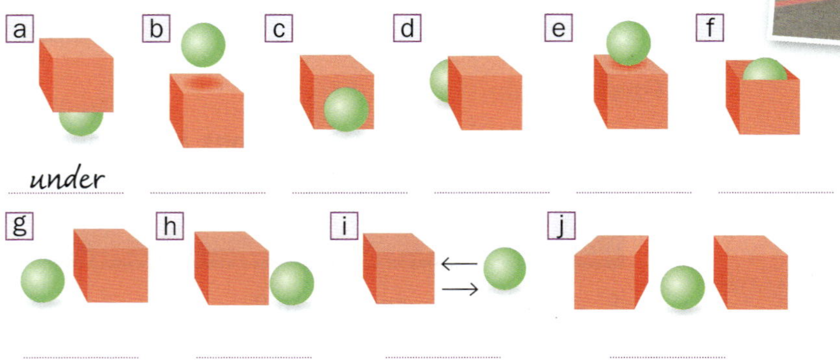

b 3.32 **Listen and check. Then listen and repeat.**

3 a Work in pairs. Describe the photos (a, b and c). What's strange about them?

b Where do you think the ball is in each photo (a–c)? Use the prepositions in Exercise 2. Put an X on the photos.

4 a 3.33 **Listen to Alan and Kayla playing 'spot the ball'. Where do they think the ball is? Do you agree?**

b Check the answers on page 141. Were Alan and Kayla right? Were *you* right?

5 3.34 **Complete the conversations with the prepositions from Exercise 2a. Then listen and check.**

Photo a

Kayla: Maybe the girl in white's got the ball (1) .... her hands. Or ... maybe it's above number ten's hand.

Alan: Yes – it's (2) .... his hand and (3) .... the net.

Photo b

Alan: Look at the position of his foot. It's on the ball. So the ball's (4) .... his foot.

Kayla: I don't know. I think the ball's (5) .... the boy and the girl, on the two lines.

Photo c

Alan: I think the boy (6) .... us is hitting the ball.

Kayla: Really? Look at the boy (7) .... him. He's waiting to hit the ball. And the boy (8) .... him in the yellow T-shirt's looking at the ball.

SPOT THE BALL 10

6 a ▶3.35 **PRONOUNCE** **Listen and repeat the /ɒ/ sound in *spot.***

b ▶3.36 **Listen and repeat these words.**

on opposite of got cross top beyond

7 **THE MOVING PICTURE** ▶ **Watch the video. Where's the ball?**

SPEAK

8 a **Work in pairs. Describe the photos. Where's the ball?**

Some people are playing …

In photo A/B I think the ball is next to / in front of / on …

b **Check your answers on page 142.**

GO BEYOND

Do the Words & Beyond exercise on page 139.

READING World sport records

>>> Read a magazine article

SPEAK AND READ

1 **Work in pairs. Look at the photos. What are the three kids doing? How old do you think they are?**

2 a 3.37 **Work in groups of three. Each student reads ONE text. Check your answers from Exercise 1. Complete the fact file for your person.**

FACT FILE >

Name: …
World record for: …
Date of record: …
Other information: …

b **Tell your partners about your person.**

PHRASE BYTES

The boy/girl in the first … photo is …

I think he's/she's …

READING TIP

Read carefully. Look for the important information (names, dates, etc).

AMAZING WORLD RECORDS

MAURICIO BALDIVIESO >

The youngest football player in a professional football team was Mauricio Baldivieso from Bolivia. He was 12 years and 362 days old when he played for Aurora FC in La Paz, Bolivia, on 19 July 2009. Mauricio's father was one of Bolivia's most famous football players and the match was an early birthday present from him. He was the team's trainer!

MIMA ITO >

Mima Ito from Japan has the world record for the biggest number of table tennis hits in one minute – she hit the ball 180 times in 60 seconds on 13 November 2011 in Tokyo. Mima started to play table tennis when she was three. In 2011 she was the youngest winner of the International Table Tennis Federation under-15 and under-18 competitions. She was 10 years old.

AARON FOTHERINGHAM >

On 24 March 2010, when he was 18, American Aaron Fotheringham set the record for the highest jump in a wheelchair. He jumped 60cm. In 2008 Aaron also set another record: he did the first jump backwards in a wheelchair. Aaron started to do tricks in his wheelchair when he was eight. For him, his wheelchair is a 'toy' and not a problem.

3 **Read all the texts again and complete the phrases.**

Mauricio play ______ a football team
Aaron do a j______ / do t______s
Mima ______ the ball
be the w______

REACT

4 **Work in pairs. What do you think of the records? Tell your partner.**

PHRASE BYTES

I like the record for …

I think … is dangerous/fantastic …

I think Aaron … is amazing / too young …

GO BEYOND

Make a list of the adjectives in the texts.

>>> Workbook, page 117

GRAMMAR Superlative adjectives

»» Compare one thing with others in a group

READ »» Grammar in context

1 Work in pairs. Read the sports records. Choose an adjective for each one.

amazing   boring   cool   hard   strange   stupid

THE WORLD'S MOST AMAZING (AND STRANGEST!) SPORTS RECORDS

THE LONGEST TIME SPINNING A BASKETBALL ON ONE FINGER: Four hours and 15 minutes (Joseph Odhiambo, 2006).

THE FASTEST 100M BY A DOG WITH A DRINKS CAN ON ITS HEAD: Two minutes and 55 seconds (Sweet Pea, 2008).

THE MOST EXPENSIVE SUMMER OLYMPIC GAMES: The 2008 Beijing Olympic Games (295 billion yuan / US$43 billion).

THE LONGEST TABLE TENNIS MATCH: 132 hours and 31 minutes (Danny Price and Randy Nunes, 1978).

STUDY

2 Complete the table with examples from Exercise 1.

Superlative adjectives	
the + short adjective + *-est*	*the stangest* ....
the most + long adjective	....
irregular superlatives	good > *best* bad > *worst* far > *furthest*

See GRAMMAR DATABASE, page 129.

Get it right

Remember: spelling can change

(See GRAMMAR DATABASE, page 129.)

strange – strangest
hot – hottest
happy – happiest

PRACTISE

3 Write the correct superlative form.

CLASS 7B: OUR CLASS RECORDS

1 Josh is *the tallest* (tall).
2 Lexi has got .... (friendly) smile.
3 Carla can do .... (amazing) drawings.
4 Blake has got .... (big) feet.
5 Violet is .... (good) at maths.
6 Vijay has got .... (fantastic) music on his music player.

4 a Write records for your class. Write sentences with the names of real students.

SUPER STUDENTS

1 is / funny
... is the funniest.
2 has got / long / hair
3 has got / exciting / pet
4 has got / cool / school bag
5 has got / nice / writing
6 has got / beautiful / name

b Work in pairs. Compare your sentences. Are they the same?

WRITE AND SPEAK

5 a Write five sentences about you, your family or your home. Choose from these adjectives.

bad   clean   dangerous   expensive
happy   horrible   interesting   noisy
old   popular   small   tidy

My brother has got the most expensive toy.

b Work in pairs. Read your sentences to your partner.

I've got the tidiest room in our house.

My grandma is the most dangerous driver in our family.

c Tell the class the most interesting thing about your partner or his/her family.

»» Workbook, pages 118–119

LISTENING AND VOCABULARY Sports camp

»» Listen to a talk

WORK WITH WORDS Sports

1 Work in pairs. Ask and answer the questions.

1 Which of these sports do you watch – basketball, football, table tennis and/or tennis?
2 Which of the sports do you play?

2 a Look at the Sports Camp website. Write the sports under the pictures (a–j).

baseball cycling golf hockey horse-riding
ice skating sailing skiing surfing volleyball

b 3.38 Listen and check. Then listen and repeat.

3 Write the sports from Exercise 2 in the correct category.

ball sports	*baseball*
water sports	
winter sports	
other sports	

LISTEN

4 3.39 Listen to the Sports Camp team leader. Order the things in his talk.

...... a story about his time at the camp
...... things to do now
...... the different sports at the camp
...... his name and job

5 3.39 Listen again and choose the correct answer (A, B or C).

1 How long is the course?
A one week
B two weeks
C three weeks
2 How many sports can students do?
A one
B three
C a different sport every day
3 What did Mason learn at Sports Camp?
A how to play volleyball
B how to play in a team
C how to make friends
4 What does Mason ask the students to do?
A say hi to other students
B ask other students questions
C go to the swimming pool
5 Where's the volleyball court?
A near the swimming pool
B in front of the students
C behind the theatre

REACT

6 Work in pairs. Answer the question and complete the tasks.

1 Do you think it's good to do a different sport each day? Why?/Why not?
2 Choose five sports you both like from Exercise 2.
3 Plan a week at Sports Camp. Which sport is best for Monday, Tuesday … ? Compare your plan with other students.

PHRASE BYTES

I think / don't think it's good because …
I like … What about you?
On Monday we can play/do …

GO BEYOND

Do the Words & Beyond exercise on page 139.

»» Workbook, pages 120–121

GRAMMAR *Be going to*

››› Talk about plans for the future

READ AND LISTEN ››› Grammar in context

1 (3.40) **Read and listen to the conversation. Which team does Lucas like – the Jets or the All-Stars?**

Zoe: Are you going to watch the game on Saturday?
Lucas: No, I'm not.
Zoe: Why not? It's the Jets and the All-Stars. Your team needs you.
Lucas: The All-Stars are a better team. I'm not going to watch them win.
Zoe: What are you going to do?
Lucas: I'm going to stay at home.
Zoe: Hannah's going to be there.
Lucas: Really?
Zoe: How sad. You aren't going to see her.

STUDY

2 Complete the table with examples from Exercise 1.

Be going to

✓ Positive
I'm going to stay at home.
Hannah ______ there.

✗ Negative
I'm not going to watch them win.
You ______ her.

? Questions
***Are** you **going to watch** the game on Saturday?*
Yes, I am. / No, ______ .
*What **are** you **going to do**?*

See GRAMMAR DATABASE, page 129.

PRACTISE

3 a Complete the sentences with *be going to* and the verbs in brackets.

1 I *'m going to walk* (walk) home after school.
2 My friends and I ______ (have) a party on Friday.
3 Our teacher ______ (not give) us homework today.
4 I ______ (play) hockey on Saturday.
5 My parents ______ (take) me to New York next summer.
6 I ______ (not come) to school tomorrow.

b Are the sentences true for you? Correct the false sentences.

1 *I'm not going to walk home after school.*

4 (3.41) **Write the correct form of *be*. Then listen and check.**

Zoe: (1) *Are* you going to come to Ali's party on Friday?
Lucas: I don't know. (2) ______ Hannah going to be there?
Zoe: Yes, she (3) ______ .
Lucas: Great. Then yes, I (4) ______ .
Zoe: What (5) ______ you going to take?
Lucas: What do you mean?
Zoe: I (6) ______ going to take some food. Hannah (7) ______ going to take some drinks.
Lucas: (8) ______ you or Hannah going to take any music?
Zoe: No, we (9) ______ .
Lucas: OK. Then I (10) ______ going to take some music.
Zoe: Cool. See you there.

5 Write the questions.

1 What / you / do / after school?
What are you going to do after school?
2 your mum / help you / with your homework?
______
3 Where / you / eat / this evening?
______
4 you / watch TV / tonight?
______
5 we / play basketball / tomorrow?
______
6 What / you / do / next weekend?
______

SPEAK

6 Work in pairs. Ask and answer the questions in Exercise 5.

What are you going to do after school?

I'm going to play the piano. What are you going to do?

I'm going to do my homework. Then I'm going to …

››› Workbook, page 122

LANGUAGE & BEYOND

>>> Do your best when things are hard

SPEAK AND READ

1 Work in pairs. Look at the pictures and answer the questions.

1 Why are the people unhappy?
2 What things are hard for *you*?

PHRASE BYTES

He/She's unhappy because …
For me it's hard to …
I can't …
I'm not very good at …

DO

2 Work in pairs. Match the advice (1–6) to the explanations (a–f).

HOW TO DO YOUR BEST WHEN THINGS ARE HARD!

1 Know your limits.
2 Take small steps.
3 Don't stop.
4 Talk to somebody.
5 Have a break.
6 Remember why.

a Try again. And again. You need time to learn new things.
b Relax. Try again later.
c Do your best. Nobody can ask for more.
d Choose a small part of the activity and do that first.
e Think about your aim. Why is this thing important to you?
f Ask for help. We all need help sometimes.

3 a Work in groups of three. Act the situation.
Student A: you have Daisy's problem. Tell your friends why you're unhappy.
Students B and C: you're Student A's friends. Give advice.

b Swap roles. First Student B has Oscar's problem. Then Student C has Amber's problem.

PHRASE BYTES

What's wrong?
I want to … but …
Don't worry. You need time …
Just do your best. Nobody can …
Relax / Choose / Think about …
That's a good idea. Thanks.

REFLECT

4 Talk about the questions. Then read the REFLECTION POINT.

1 What things do people find hard?
2 How do you feel when you can do something hard?
3 What's the best advice in Exercise 2?

REFLECTION POINT

Everybody finds something hard. When things are hard, don't be unhappy. Try again. And remember: you can only do your best.

EXTEND

5 Think of something that's hard for you. Choose advice from Exercise 2. Then tell a partner your problem and what you're going to do.

SCHOOL SKILLS

Workbook, page 125

SPEAKING Where is it?

10

›››› Ask for and give directions

SPEAK

1 Work in groups. Ask and answer the questions.

1 When was the last time you gave somebody directions?
2 Where were you? Where did the person want to go?
3 Did you give the directions in English or in your language?

WATCH OR LISTEN

2 3.42 Watch or listen to the scenes. Why is Zac going to the theatre?

1

Zac: Excuse me. How do I (1) .... to the Cornerstone theatre?
Jiya: (2) .... straight on and (3) .... the second street on the left. It's on the right.
Zac: Thank you.

2

Zac: Excuse me. Where are the toilets?
Kelly: (4) .... up the stairs and (5) .... right. They're next to the café.
Zac: Thanks.

3

Zac: Excuse me. Where's the studio? I've got a dance class.
Kent: (6) .... through that door and (7) .... left. The studio's at the end on the left.

3 3.42 Complete the conversations with the verbs in the box. Then watch or listen again and check your answers.

get   go (x3)   take   turn (x2)

4 a Complete the directions with one word. Use the conversations to help you.

1 Go .... on.

2 Turn ....

3 Go .... the stairs.

b Complete the sentences with words from Exercise 4a.

1 The opposite of *right* is ....
2 The opposite of *down* is ....

5 3.43 Listen and repeat the questions and directions.

ACT

6 Work in pairs. Complete the tasks.

- Choose two places in the box.
- Take it in turns to ask for and give directions to the places.
- Present your conversations to other students, but don't say the places. Can they guess where you want to go?

the café or shop   the library   the sports centre or gym
the teachers' room   the toilets

PHRASEBOOK 3.44

Ask for directions

Excuse me, …
Where's / Where are … ?
How do I get to … ?
Thank you. / Thanks.

Give directions

Go straight on.
Go down/up the stairs.
Go through the café / that door.
Turn left/right.
Take the first/second street on the left/right.
It's/They're next to / in front of …
It's on the left / at the end.

›››› Workbook, page 123

WRITING Latest update

>>> Write a blog post

SPEAK AND READ

1 Work in pairs. Ask and answer the questions.

Do you read messages on websites or blogs? → YES: Which ones? Do you ever post messages?
→ NO: Why not?

2 Read the blog post. (Don't worry about the mistakes!)
What part of the world does Sam live in – the north or the south?

MY BLOG

HOME ABOUT

18TH DECEMBER — POSTED BY: SAM

Three things that I'm going to do this summer

1 I'm going to go sufring every day.
(And live on the beach with my friends!)

2 We're going to break the world record for the longest game of beach volleyball
(31st December at 10am on Long Beach. Are you going to help?)

3 Im going to spend a week in madagascar.
(Definitely going to be my best holiday ever.)

3 Read the tips in the HOW TO box. Then find and correct the four mistakes in the blog post.

HOW TO
check your writing

- Check apostrophes and capital letters (see pages 28 and 50).
- Check your spelling (see page 94).
- Check there's a full stop (.) at the end of each sentence.
- Check your grammar:
  Tenses – past, present, future
  Verb forms – *do, doing, to do*
  Superlatives – *the hottest day*

PRACTISE

4 Find and correct three mistakes in each plan for the summer.

1 I'm going continue with my guitar classes
(I have my first class last week!)

2 I'm going to wach cycling (the *Tour de France*) on TV.
(Best cyclists in the world going to be in it.)

3 Were going to visit my grandparents in italy.
(I get ready for the trip now.)

PLAN

5 You're going to write a blog post about your summer plans. Use the *Writing plan* to help you prepare.

WRITING PLAN

1 **Think about your plans.**
What are you going to do this summer?
Think of three things. ☐

2 **Write a comment on each plan.**
Put some extra information in brackets ( ). ☐

3 **Check your post.**
Read the tips in the HOW TO box. ☐

WRITE AND CHECK

6 Write your blog post. Then check it. Tick (✓) the things in the plan.

SHARE

7 Swap your blog post with other students. Who has the best summer plans? Why?

Workbook, pages 124–125

VOCABULARY Prepositions of place

1 Look at the poster. Complete the description with the words in the box.

The 8th Summer Games

above	behind	between	in	in front
near	next	on	opposite	under

The tennis court's (1) ________ the beach. Two players are (2) ________ the court. The boy's standing (3) ________ the girl. The net's (4) ________ the two players and (5) ________ of the girl. The ball's (6) ________ the girl's head and her racket's (7) ________ her hand. There's a white line (8) ________ her feet. There's a man on a chair (9) ________ to the net and some people (10) ________ him.

___ /10

Sports

2 Complete the sports in the programme.

THE PARK / THE BEACH
Saturday morning
tennis
(1) g _ _ f
(2) su _ _ _ _ g
Saturday afternoon
(3) cy _ _ _ _ g
(4) ho _ _ _ y
(5) vo _ _ _ _ _ _ _ l
Sunday morning
(6) ba _ _ _ _ _ l
(7) ho _ _ e-ri _ _ _ g
(8) sa _ _ _ _ g
REMEMBER!
(9) sk _ _ _ g and
(10) ic _ sk _ _ _ g are on the programme for our 1st Winter Games.

___ /10

GRAMMAR Superlative adjectives

3 Complete the advert with superlative adjectives.

Come to the 8th Summer Games – the (1) ________ (**good**) sports event of the year. This summer we have our (2) ________ (**big**) selection of sports competitions ever. Come and see the (3) ________ (**fast**) runners, the (4) ________ (**exciting**) players and the (5) ________ (**famous**) local stars in action. Watch local teenager Mark Warner do the (6) ________ (**amazing**) tricks in his wheelchair. And see it all in the company of the country's (7) ________ (**friendly**) people!

___ /14

Be going to

4 Complete the radio interview with *be going to* and short answers.

Don: So Claire, tell us about this year's Summer Games.
Claire: They (1) ________ (**be**) really big, Don. People (2) ________ (**come**) from all over the country.
Don: (3) ________ (**you/take**) part in the games this year, Claire?
Claire: Yes, I (4) ________ . I (5) ________ (**celebrate**) my 40th birthday next month, but my age (6) ________ (**not stop**) me!
Don: (7) ________ (**Janet/play**) in the tennis competition? Your daughter's a great player.
Claire: No, she (8) ________ . I … er … didn't remember to send in the form … Maybe next year.

___ /16

Your score: ___ /50

SKILLS CHECK

✓✓✓ Yes, I can. No problem!
✓✓ Yes, I can. But I need a bit of help.
✓ Yes, I can. But I need a lot of help.

I can read a magazine article. ____
I can listen to a talk. ____
I can do my best when things are hard. ____
I can ask for and give directions. ____
I can write a blog post. ____

Workbook, pages 126–127

READ

1 Complete the conversation between Selina and her mum. Write the correct letter (A–H) for the gaps (1–5).

EXAM TIPS

match sentences to gaps in a conversation

- Read the conversation with the gaps. What's it about?
- Decide what kind of information is missing.
- Read the eight choices (A–H). Match them to the correct gaps. Look at the example.
- You only need to use five of the choices.

Example:

Mum: Where did you last see your diary?

Selina: (0) E

Mum: Did you write in it yesterday?

Selina: (1) ___

Mum: Maybe you put it in the cupboard.

Selina: (2) ___

Mum: Well, what about under your bed?

Selina: (3) ___

Mum: Selina, what's that there?

Selina: (4) ___

Mum: Between your bed and the wall.

Selina: (5) ___

Mum: I think it's time to tidy your room.

A Oh, it's my diary.

B No, there are only dirty clothes under there.

C It's in front of you.

D But I never put it in there.

E I don't know. I can't remember.

F It's blue and it says DON'T READ on it.

G No, I didn't. I was too tired.

H What? Where?

Reading: ______ /10

LISTEN

2 3.45 **Listen to an announcement by a headteacher. Complete the notes.**

School announcement

About: after-school sports (0) *clubs*

Sports offered: basketball, (1) ________ , dancing, hockey and volleyball

Which students: in Years (2) ________

Start: (3) ________ September

Club lists: (4) in the school ________

Skiing trip information: (5) on the school ________

Listening: ______ /10

WRITE

3 Complete Jack's email to his pen pal Dan. For questions 1–10, write one word for each space.

New mail Reply Forward

Dear Dan,

Thanks for your email. You asked (0) *about* last week. Well, Monday and Tuesday (1) ________ really boring. I didn't (2) ________ much then – just school and homework. On Wednesday I (3) ________ volleyball in the school team. The match was (4) ________ hardest match this year and we didn't (5) ________ . On Friday I stayed (6) ________ home (7) ________ I was ill. At the weekend I practised the piano. I'm (8) ________ to take a piano exam next week. What about you? (9) ________ you have a good week? What (10) ________ you going to do next week?

Best wishes,
Jack

Writing: ______ / 10

Progress check score ______ /30

EXAM TIPS

listen and complete notes

- Read the information before you listen.
- Look at the example.
- Decide what type of information you need (names, numbers, …).
- Listen for this information. Write the numbers or words.
- When you listen again, check your answers.

use important words to help you listen
See page 102

EXAM TIPS

complete a text with gaps

- First read the text quickly.
- Look at the words before and after each gap.
- Use only one word in the gap.
- Use the correct form of the verbs. Check your spelling.

use *because*
See page 106

check your writing
See page 116

I/my, you/your

Personal pronouns and possessive adjectives

	Personal pronouns	Possessive adjectives
Singular	I	my
	you	your
	he	his
	she	her
	it	its
Plural	we	our
	you	your
	they	their

Be

- Notice how we use the verb *be*:
  Hi, I'm Sarah.
  He isn't in our class.
  Where are your parents from?

Positive

I'm
You're
He's / She's / It's
We're / They're

Negative

I'm not
You aren't
He/She/It isn't
We/They aren't

Questions and short answers

Am I … ?	Yes, you are. / No, you're not.
Are you … ?	Yes, I am. / No, I'm not.
Is he … ?	Yes, he is. / No, he isn't.
Is she … ?	Yes, she is. / No, she isn't.
Is it … ?	Yes, it is. / No, it isn't.
Are we … ?	Yes, you are. / No, you're not.
Are they … ?	Yes, they are. /No, they aren't.

Plural nouns

- Add -s to most nouns in the plural:
  games, films, hotels
- Add -es to nouns ending in *-ch, -sh, -s, -ss* or *-x*:
  buses, classes, lunches, boxes
- For nouns ending in a consonant (eg *n, t*) and *y*, change *y* to *i* and add *-es*: *city – cities*
- For nouns ending in a vowel (eg *a, e*) and *y*, add -s: *key – keys*
- The following nouns are always plural:
  jeans, sunglasses, scissors
- The following nouns have irregular plural forms:
  *man – **men*** *person – **people***
  *woman – **women*** *child – **children***

a/an, the

USE

- Use *a/an* when you mention a noun for the first time:
  *I like **an** ice cream on a hot day.*
- Use *a/an* with nouns for jobs and occupations:
  *We've got **a** great maths teacher.*
- Use *the* before a specific thing:
  ***The** school bus is late.*
- Use *the* before something there is only one of:
  *I love **the** internet.*
- Use no article when talking about things in general:
  I don't like video games.

FORM

- Use *a* before nouns beginning with consonants:
  a bus
- Use *an* before nouns beginning with vowels:
  an ice cream

This/that, these/those

	Here	There
Singular	this	that
Plural	these	those

- Use *this* to talk about one thing here:
  What's this?
- Use *these* to talk about more than one thing here: *These bananas are nice.*
- Use *that* to talk about one thing there:
  That apple is red.
- Use *those* to talk about more than one thing there: *I like those sunglasses.*

Have got

USE

- Use *have got* to talk about possession:
  *I've **got** one brother.*
  *I **haven't got** a tablet.*
  *Sam**'s got** a computer.*
  ***Have** you **got** a favourite TV programme?*

FORM

Positive

I've **got**	a big family.
You've **got**	
He's/She's/It's **got**	
We've **got**	
They've **got**	

- *'ve got* and *'s got* are the short forms of *have got* and *has got*. You usually use the short forms in informal English.

Negative

I **haven't got**	a mobile phone.
You **haven't got**	
He/She/It **hasn't got**	
We **haven't got**	
They **haven't got**	

- You often use *any* with the negative forms of *have got* and plural nouns:
  *I haven't got **any apples**.*

Questions and short answers

Have	I/you/we/they	**got** a tablet?
Has	he/she/it	**got** a mobile phone?

Yes,	you/I/we/they	**have.**
	he/she/it	**has.**
No,	you/I/we/they	**haven't.**
	he/she/it	**hasn't.**

- You often use *any* before plural nouns with the question forms of *have got*:
  *Have you got **any** brothers or sisters?*

WATCH OUT! You never use short forms in positive short answers:
Yes, I have. (not ~~*Yes, I've.*~~)

Whose?; possessive *'s/s'* and possessive pronouns

Whose? and possessive *'s/s'*

USE

- Use possessive *'s* and *whose* to talk about possessions or relationships:
  ***Whose** phone is this?*
  *It's my sister**'s**. (The phone belongs to my sister.)*
  ***Whose** keys are these?*
  *They're my dad**'s**.*

FORM

- Use singular noun + *'s*:
  It's my sister's phone. (sister + 's + phone)
- Use regular plural noun + *s'*:
  *That's my grandparent**s'** house over there. (grandparent + s' + house)*
- Use *'s* for irregular plural nouns such as *children, people, women, men*:
  *The children**'s** books were all over the floor.*

WATCH OUT! Notice the difference between possessive *'s* and the short form of ***is*** – *'s*:
*Is that Jacob**'s** bag?*
*Jacob**'s** 14 years old.*

Possessive pronouns

USE

- Use a possessive pronoun in place of a possessive adjective (*my, your*) + noun:
  *It's her book. It's **hers**.*
  *That's my phone. It's **mine**.*

FORM

Possessive adjectives	Possessive pronouns
my	mine
your	yours
his/her	his/hers
our	ours
their	theirs

Imperatives and object pronouns

Imperatives

USE

- Use imperatives to give instructions and commands:
  Give *them food and water every day.*
  Come *into the classroom and* ***sit*** *down.*

FORM

- Form the imperative with the base form of the verb:
  Open *the window.*
  Close *the door.*
- Use *don't* before the verb to tell someone not to do something:
  Shhhh! ***Don't talk.***
  Don't forget *to give them food and water.*

Object pronouns

USE

- Use object pronouns after verbs:
  Listen to ***me.***
  Give ***them*** *food and water every day.*
  Don't put ***her*** *in your room.*

FORM

Subject pronouns	Object pronouns
I	me
you	you
he	him
she	her
it	it
we	us
you	you
they	them

There is / there are

USE

- Use *there is / there are* to describe what's in a place:
  In my classroom ***there's*** *a big clock.*
  There isn't *a computer.*
  There are *some pictures on the wall.*
  Is there *a table?*

FORM

Positive

There's a desk.
There are some chairs.

- *There's* is the short form of *there is.* You usually use the short form in informal English.
- You often use *some* with *there are* before plural nouns.

Negative

There isn't a computer.
There aren't any windows.

- You often use *any* with *there aren't* before plural nouns.
- *There isn't* and *there aren't* are the short forms of *there is not* and *there are not.* You usually use the short forms in informal English.

Questions and short answers

Is there a clock?	Yes, **there is.** / No, **there isn't.**
Are there any pictures?	Yes, **there is.** / No, **there aren't.**

Can/can't

USE

- Use *can/can't* to talk about the things we have the ability or time to do:
  *I **can** play tennis.*
  *I **can't** hear very well.*

FORM

- The form stays the same. *Can and can't* are the same for *I*, *you*, *he/she/it*, *we* and *they*.

I	**can/can't**	see you.
You		
He/She/It		
We		
They		

Questions and short answers

- Form questions by changing the word order:
  ***Can you** play the guitar?*

Can	I/you/we/they	swim?	Yes, I/you/we/they **can**.
			No, I/you/we/they **can't**.
	he/she/it		Yes, he/she/it **can**.
			No, he/she/it **can't**.

Present simple

USE

Use the present simple to talk about

- things that are generally true:
  *My sister **plays** the violin.*
  *Max **writes** the songs for our group.*
- habits and routines:
  *I **practise** the piano every day.*
  *We **watch** television in the evening.*

FORM

Positive

- The present simple for *I, you, we* and *they* is the same. For the *he/she/it* forms, add *-s, -es* or *-ies* to the verb.

I/You/We/They	**read**	a lot of books.
He/She/It	**plays**	football every weekend.

Spelling: *he/she/it* forms

- If a verb ends in *-ch*, *-s*, *-sh*, *-x* or *-o*, add *-es*:
  *My aunt **teaches** English at a school.*
  *Ingrid **goes** to a music club after school.*
- If a verb ends in a consonant and *-y*, change the *-y* into *-i* and add *-es*:
  *My brother **studies** Spanish.*

Present simple

FORM

Negative

- Form the present simple negative with *don't* (*do not*) or *doesn't* (*does not*) + verb.

I/You/We/They	**don't**	watch television	in the morning.
He/She/It	**doesn't**	play football	after school.

WATCH OUT! In negative sentences don't add **-*s*** to the verb after ***doesn't***:
He doesn't ***speak*** *French.* (not ~~*He doesn't speaks French.*~~)

Questions and short answers

- Form questions in the present simple with *do/does* + subject + verb.

Do	I/you/we/they	**believe** her?
Does	he/she/it	**work** in a school?

Yes,	I/you/we/they	**do.**
	he/she/it	**does.**
No,	I/you/we/they	**don't.**
	he/she/it	**doesn't.**

Question words

- To ask questions in the present simple, use a question word (*where, who, what, when, how, which, why*) + *do/does* + subject + verb:
  When do you go to bed?
  How do you travel to school?

Adverbs of frequency

USE

- Use adverbs of frequency to say how often you do things:
  I ***usually*** *go to school by bus.*
  We ***sometimes*** *watch films in the evenings.*
  My sister ***never*** *gets up early.*

- The main adverbs of frequency are (in order of frequency):

0% never
sometimes
often
usually
100% always

- Adverbs of frequency usually go **before** the main verb:
  I ***sometimes help*** *my dad with the cooking.*
- Adverbs of frequency go **after** *am/are/is/can*:
  *Her room****'s always*** *in a mess.*
- Look at where the adverbs go in these questions:
  What time do you ***usually*** *get up?*
  How ***often*** *do you have lunch at school?*

Comparative adjectives

USE

- Use comparative adjectives to compare two things:
  New York is **bigger than** *Washington DC.*
  New York is **more dangerous than** *Washington DC.*

FORM

- To form the comparative of most adjectives, add *-er.*
- Most longer adjectives (eg *expensive*) add *more* before the adjective:
  London is **more** *expensive than Manchester.*
- See the table for other spelling changes.
- Use *than* after the comparative adjective:
  Washington DC is safer **than** *New York.*

Word type	Adjective	Comparative adjective
One syllable	clean	clean**er**
One syllable ending in *-e*	safe	safe**r**
One syllable ending in one vowel + one consonant	big	big**ger**
Two syllables ending in *-y*	dirty	dirt**ier**
Two or more syllables	expensive	**more** expensive
Two or more syllables ending in *-er, -et, -ow* or *-le*	quiet	quiet**er**

WATCH OUT! Some comparative adjectives are irregular.

Adjective	Comparative adjective
good	better
bad	worse
far	further

Some and *any*, *much* and *many*

Countable nouns

- are nouns you can count:
  fact, vegetable, chip, etc
- use *a(n)* or *the* in the singular:
  I usually eat an apple every day.
- have a singular and a plural form:
  lemon *lemons*

Uncountable nouns

- are nouns you can't count:
  meat, cheese, pasta, etc
- don't have a plural from:
  I like a lot of **cheese** *on my pasta.*
- You can't say *one meat, two meats*, etc.
- Some more common uncountable nouns are:
  food, salad, bread, spaghetti, soup, milk, juice, fruit, rice
- Some nouns can be both countable and uncountable:
  How much ice cream do Italians eat?
  Would you like an ice cream?

some

USE

- Use *some* to describe an amount that is not big and not small. You can use *some* with countable and uncountable nouns:
  We've got **some bananas.**
  There's **some juice** *in the fridge.*
- You can also use *some* when making offers or requests with countable and uncountable nouns:
  Would you like **some chips**?
  Can I have **some pasta**?

any

USE

- Use *any* in negative sentences to talk about zero amounts. You can use *any* with both countable and uncountable nouns:
  There aren't **any vegetables.**
  We haven't got **any bread.**
- Use *any* with countable and uncountable nouns to ask about quantity:
  Have we got **any milk**?
  Are there **any eggs** *in the fridge?*

much and *many*

USE

- Use *How many* or *How much* to ask about quantity. Use *How many* for countable nouns and *How much* for uncountable nouns:
  How many *minutes do you cook pasta for?*
  How much *pasta do Italians eat?*
- Use *not* + *many* with countable nouns and *not* + *much* with uncountable nouns to talk about a small amount of something in negative sentences:
  Italians don't each **much** *meat.*
  There aren't **many** *eggs in the fridge.*

Present continuous

USE

- Use the present continuous to talk about things in progress now or around now:
  What ***are you doing****?*
  I'm watching *television.*
  *It's very sunny so my brother****'s wearing*** *sunglasses.*
- You often use time expressions such as *now, today* and *at the moment* with the present continuous:
  I'm not studying ***today****. It's a holiday.*

FORM

Positive

- Form the present continuous with *be* + *-ing* form of the verb.

I'**m** You'**re** He'**s**/She'**s**	**wearing**	trainers.
It'**s**	**raining.**	
We'**re** They'**re**	**sleeping.**	

- You usually use the short forms of *be* in the present continuous:
  *He****'s riding*** *his bike.*

Spelling

- If a verb ends in *-e*, remove the final *-e* before adding *-ing*:
  take – taking *use – using*
- If a verb ends in a vowel (eg *i, a, o*) and a consonant (eg *m, p, t*), double the consonant before adding *-ing:*
  swim – swimming *shop – shopping*
- If a verb ends in *-l*, double the *-l* before adding *-ing:*
  travel – travelling
- If a verb ends in *-ie*, change the *-ie* to *-ying*:
  lie – lying

Negative

- Form the present continuous negative with *be* + *not* + *-ing* form of the verb.

I'm not You **aren't** He **isn't**/She **isn't**	**watching**	a video.
It **isn't**	**working.**	
We **aren't** They **aren't**	**meeting**	friends.

Questions and short answers

- Form present continuous questions with *be* + subject + *-ing* form of the verb.

Am	I	**listening** to music?	Yes, you **are.** / No, you**'re not.**
Are	you		Yes, I **am.** / No, I**'m not.**
Is	he/she	**making** a cake?	Yes, he/she **is.** / No, he/she **isn't.**
	it	**raining?**	Yes, it **is.** / No, it **isn't.**
Are	we/they	**having** a party?	Yes, we/they **are.** / No, we/they **aren't.**

- You can also use question words (*What, Why, Who, Where, How*, etc) before *be*:
  What are you doing *here?*
  Why are you wearing *a shirt and jacket?*
  Where ***are you going****?*

WATCH OUT! You never use short forms in positive short answers:
Yes, ***I am.*** (not ~~*Yes, I'm.*~~)

Was/were

USE

- Use the past simple of *be* to talk about situations in the past:
  *I **was** in a play on Saturday. My parents **were** in the audience.*
  *My sister **wasn't** at school yesterday.*

FORM

Positive

- The positive form of the past simple of *be* is *was* or *were*.

I/He/She/It	**was**	late for school.
You/We/They	**were**	

Negative

- The negative form of the past simple of *be* is *wasn't* or *weren't*.

I/He/She/It	**wasn't** (was not)	at school yesterday.
You/We/They	**weren't** (were not)	

Questions and short answers

- To form questions, use *was/were* + subject.

Were you	at the pool yesterday?	Yes, I **was**. No, I **wasn't**.
Was he/she/it		Yes, he/she/it **was**. No, he/she/it **wasn't**.
Were we/they		Yes, we/they **were**. No, we/they **weren't**.

- You often use these time expressions with *was/were*:

yesterday, at the weekend, on Saturday, last Sunday/weekend/week

Past simple

USE

- Use the past simple to talk about completed actions in the past:
  *Yesterday I **went** to the beach and **swam** in the sea.*
  *In the evening I **ate** dinner and **watched** TV.*

- You often use these time expressions with the past simple:

yesterday	last night/week/month/year	
on Monday	in October	in 2013

FORM

Regular verbs

- Form the past simple of regular verbs with verb + *ed*. It is the same for all persons.

I/You/He/She/It/We/They	**hated** it.

Spelling

- If a verb ends in *-y*, change the *y* into *i* before adding *-ed*:
  *study – stud**ied***
- But not if there is a vowel before the *-y*:
  *play – play**ed*** (not ~~*plaid*~~)
- If a verb ends in a vowel (eg *o*) and a consonant (eg *p*, *t*), double the consonant:
  *stop – sto**pped***
- If a verb ends in *-l*, double the *l*:
  *travel – trave**lled***

Irregular verbs

- Many verbs are irregular in the past simple. You have to learn these.
  *buy – **bought***   *come – **came***   *go – **went***

(See page 140 for a list of irregular verbs in the past simple.)

Past simple

FORM

Negative

- Form the negative past simple with *didn't* (*did not*) + verb.

I/You/He/ She/We/ They	**didn't** (did not)	**go**	to school yesterday.

- Use the short form *didn't* in informal speech and writing.
- The past simple negative is the same for regular and irregular verbs.

Questions and short answers

USE

- Use the past simple to ask about completed actions in the past:
__Did__ you __have__ a good day?
__Did__ you __have__ breakfast this morning?

FORM

- Form past simple questions with *Did* + subject + verb.

Did	you/he/she/it/we/they	**have** a good time?
Yes,	I/you/he/she/it/we/they	**did.**
No,	I/you/he/she/it/we/they	**didn't.**

- You can also use question words (*What, Who, Where, How,* etc) before *did*:
__Where did you go__ last night?

WATCH OUT! Don't use the past form in negatives and questions:
I didn't __watch__ TV last night. (not *I ~~didn't **watched**~~ TV last night.*)
Did you __take__ a lot of photos? (not *~~Did you **took**~~ a lot of photos?*)

Superlative adjectives

USE

- Use superlative adjectives to compare one thing with all the other things in a group:
  *Martin is **the youngest** person in our class.*
  *But he is also **the tallest**!*

FORM

- To form the superlative of most adjectives use *the* + adjective + *-est*. See the table for other spelling changes.

Word type	Adjective	Superlative adjective
One syllable	fast	**the** fast**est**
One syllable ending in *-e*	late	**the** late**st**
One syllable ending in one vowel + one consonant	big	**the** big**gest**
Two syllables ending in *-y*	friendly	**the** friendl**iest**
Two or more syllables	expensive	**the most** expensive
Two or more syllables ending in *-er*, *-et*, *-ow* or *-le*	clever	**the** clever**est**

WATCH OUT! Some superlative adjectives are irregular.

Adjective	Superlative adjective
good	the best
bad	the worst
far	the furthest

Be going to

USE

- Use *be going to* + verb to talk about plans in the future:
  I'm going to *visit my grandad this weekend.*
  We're going to *watch the fireworks this evening.*
  *What **are you going to do** after school?*

FORM

Positive

I'm	**going to**	meet my friends tomorrow.
You're/We're/They're		
He's/She's/It's		

Negative

I'm **not**	**going to**	watch the game.
You/We/They **aren't**		
He/She/It **isn't**		

Questions and short answers

Form questions with *be* + subject + *going to* + verb.

Am I	going to	come to the party?	**Yes**, I **am**. **No**, I**'m not**.
Is he/she/it			**Yes**, he/she/it **is**. **No**, he/she/it **isn't**.
Are you/we/they			**Yes**, you/we/they **are**. **No**, you/we/they **aren't**.

WORDS & BEYOND

UNIT 1

Page 10

RECALL

A–Z WORDS

address
bike
car
dinosaur
elephant
football
group
homework
ice cream
jeans
key
lunch
metro
notebook
orange
phone
question
room
sunglasses
T-shirt
us
video
website
Xbox
you
zoo

WORK WITH WORDS

TIP: Make a dictionary. Write new words with the same first letter together.

TASK: Choose a letter and write five words under it. Next to each word, write the word in your language.

Pages 10 and 11

CATEGORIES

animals
clothes
food
games
home
people
school
technology
transport

GO BEYOND

Make a *likes* ☺ and *dislikes* ☹ list. Add one word from each category to your lists.

Page 14

COUNTRIES AND NATIONALITIES

Brazil	Brazilian
Germany	German
Italy	Italian
Japan	Japanese
South Africa	South African
Turkey	Turkish

GO BEYOND

Think of a famous person or place for each country. Write a sentence.

… *is from/in* [country].
… *is* [nationality].

1 ....
2 ....
3 ....
4 ....
5 ....
6 ....

OTHER IMPORTANT WORDS

album
alphabet
apple
article
bad
big
bin
boring
card
category
chair
city
classmate
computer
cool
drink
eat
favourite
fridge
fruit salad
glass
grape
great
holiday
horrible
international
label
match
mountain bike
neighbour
new
nice
noisy
old
point
postcards
quiet
rap
rubbish
Russia
sandwich
similar
small
something
stay (in a hotel)
story
the same
the UK
the USA
thing
tourist
visit

Page 20

RECALL

OPPOSITE ADJECTIVES

bad	good
big	small
nice	horrible
noisy	quiet
old	new/young
same	different

WORK WITH WORDS

TIP: Learn opposites together.

TASK: Find opposites for these words in the unit: *wrong* – … , *easy* – … .

Pages 20 and 21

FAMILY

brother
dad
father
grandad
grandchild
grandfather
grandma
grandmother
mother
mum
only child
sister

GO BEYOND

Make a family tree for you with these family words.

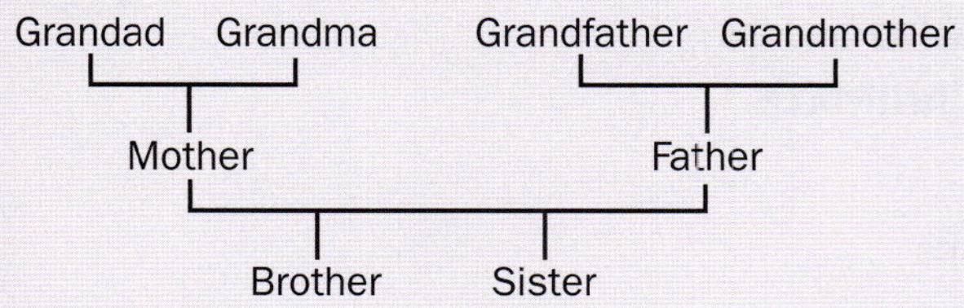

Page 24

PARTS OF THE BODY

arm
back
ear
eye
face
foot
hand
head
leg
mouth
nose
teeth

GO BEYOND

Touch and say the parts of your body in the list.

OTHER IMPORTANT WORDS

camera
clever
contact list
easy
fantastic
friendly
hard
holiday
idea
in the middle
laptop
like (adv)
morning
on the right/left
pen
player
present
problem
repeat
smile
special
spell
street
tablet
text message
time
today
wrong number

WORDS & BEYOND

UNIT 3

Page 32

RECALL

PARTS OF THE BODY

arm
back
ear
eye
face
head
leg
mouth
nose
teeth

WORK WITH WORDS

TIP: Draw pictures to help you remember new words.

TASK: Draw pictures of the parts of the body.

Pages 32 and 33

PET ANIMALS

bird
cat
chicken
dog
fish
hamster
horse
mouse
rabbit
sheep

GO BEYOND

Match these adjectives to the pet animals:

big
horrible
nice
noisy
quiet
small
tall

Page 36

THINGS IN YOUR ROOM

Parts of a room

door
floor
wall
window

Furniture

bed
chair
desk
table

Other things

clock
computer
light
picture

GO BEYOND

Add one more word to each category. Use a dictionary to help you.

OTHER IMPORTANT WORDS

adopt
basketball
Britain
borrow
box
cartoon
cross (v)
egg
fetch
fridge
grass
lunch
neighbour
order
popular
postcard
quickly
quiet
Scottish
shake hands
stay
survey
tall
tidy
the United States
wait

Page 42

RECALL

FREE-TIME WORDS

bike
book
cinema
football
friends
internet
music
shopping
television
video games

WORK WITH WORDS

TIP: Write a translation (= the word in your language) for new words. Note if the translation is the same, similar or different.

TASK: Write a translation for the RECALL words. Then write *the same*, *similar* or *different* next to the translations.

Pages 42 and 43

FREE-TIME ACTIVITIES

go shopping
go to the cinema
go on the internet
listen to music
meet friends
play football
play video games
read a book
ride my bike
watch television

GO BEYOND

Choose five activities. Write a sentence to say when you do them.

Page 46

MUSIC

Musical instruments

drums
guitar
keyboard
piano
violin

Types of music

classical
hip hop
Latin
pop
rock

GO BEYOND

Match some of the words to a famous person or group.

OTHER IMPORTANT WORDS

audio book
blind
board
dance
dark
deaf
diary
disability
guess
headings
hearing aid
homework
influence
interview
light (adj)
make a note of
nervous
piece of paper
play (n)
sign language
sing
singer
title
wheelchair

Page 54

RECALL

PLACES

farm
football club
hospital
hotel
restaurant
school
shop
theatre

WORK WITH WORDS

TIP: Think of places and people you know.

TASK: How many of the places are there in your town? Make a list and write the names of the places. Do you know people who work in any of the places?

Pages 54 and 55

JOBS

actor
cook
doctor
farmer
football player
nurse
receptionist
shop assistant
teacher
waiter/waitress

GO BEYOND

Choose five jobs. Write one thing that each person needs.

waiter – a menu

Page 58

DAILY ACTIVITIES

do my homework
finish school
get up
go home
go to bed
go to school
have a shower
have breakfast
have dinner
have lunch

GO BEYOND

Write your daily routine backwards. Start with the last thing you do and end with the first thing. Don't look at the list of words.

I go to bed …

OTHER IMPORTANT WORDS

active
carefully
daily routine
drive
ice cream
mystery
normal
order (food in a restaurant)
questionnaire
radio show
smile
website post

Page 64

RECALL

THINGS IN YOUR ROOM

bed
chair
clock
computer
desk
door
floor
light
picture
table
wall
window

WORK WITH WORDS

TIP: Close your eyes and 'see' a place in your head. 'Say' the words in your head for all the things in English.

TASK: Close your eyes and 'see' your room at home. 'Say' the words in your head.

Pages 64 and 65

HOME

apartment
balcony
bathroom
bedroom
dining room
flat
garden
hall
house
kitchen
living room
swimming pool

GO BEYOND

Write two sentences about your favourite room in your home. Say why you like it.

Page 68

FOOD AND DRINK

apple
banana
bread
cheese
chicken
coffee
egg
fish
fruit
fruit salad
grapes
ice cream
juice
lemon
meat
milk
oil
pasta
pizza
rice
salad
sandwich
steak
tea
vegetables
watermelon

GO BEYOND

Write a menu with your favourite food and drinks.

OTHER IMPORTANT WORDS

any
Asia
boat
capital (city)
clean
comfortable
course
cupboard
dangerous
dirty
Europe
expensive
fact
far
freezer
fridge
How much is it?
kilo
many
meal
much
the Netherlands
safe
some
souvenir
swap
tall
tent
view

WORDS & BEYOND

UNIT 7

Page 76

RECALL

COLOURS

black
blue
brown
green
orange
pink
purple
red
white
yellow

CLOTHES AND ACCESSORIES

bag
jeans
sunglasses
T-shirt

WORK WITH WORDS

TIP: Use colours to organise vocabulary. Write nouns in one colour, adjectives in another colour, verbs in another, etc.

TASK: Write *Nouns*, *Verbs* and *Adjectives* at the top of a piece of paper in different colours. Write four words under each title in the same colours.

Pages 76 and 77

CLOTHES

dress
hat
jacket
shirt
shoes
skirt
socks
sweatshirt
trainers
trousers

GO BEYOND

What clothes have you got? How many? Make a list and include colours.

I've got a / some / a lot of …

Page 80

ACTION VERBS

carry
chat
dance
drive
fly
point
run
shop
sit
stand
swim
wait

GO BEYOND

Use the verbs to write six sentences about things you *always*, *often*, *sometimes* and *never* do.

OTHER IMPORTANT WORDS

accessories
castle
cola
go out
king
mime
play (n)
polite
prince
queen
scene
sign
stripes
Wow!

Page 86

RECALL

COUNTRIES

Argentina
Australia
Brazil
Chile
Germany
Italy
Japan
Mexico
Russia
South Africa
the USA
Turkey

CONTINENTS

Africa
Asia
Australia
Europe
North America
South America

WORK WITH WORDS

TIP: Make a note of word stress: *Argentina*.

TASK: Make a note of word stress in the names of other countries. Use your dictionary for help.

Pages 86 and 87

WEATHER

cloudy
cold
cool
dry
foggy
hot
raining
snowing
sunny
warm
windy
wet

GO BEYOND

Choose six words to describe the weather. Write a place (town, city, country or continent) where each type of weather is normal.

Page 90

THE COUNTRY

beach
island
mountain
river
sea
sky
town
tree
village
wood

GO BEYOND

Are there any of these places where you live? Write their names.

OTHER IMPORTANT WORDS

audience
autumn
break
careful
cent
change
count
day off school
day out
dry season
euro
long-term memory
maths
memory
picnic
rainy season
roller coaster
season
snack
spring
summer
tip
weather alert
weather report
winter
working memory

Page 98

RECALL

DAYS AND MONTHS

Days of the week

Monday
Tuesday
Wednesday
Thursday
Friday
Saturday
Sunday

Months of the year

January
February
March
April
May
June
July
August
September
October
November
December

WORK WITH WORDS

TIP: Learn words in groups. **TASK:** Say the words in these groups: (1) seasons, (2) continents.

Pages 98 and 99

DATES

1st first
2nd second
3rd third
4th fourth
5th fifth
6th sixth
7th seventh
8th eighth
9th ninth
10th tenth
11th eleventh
12th twelfth
13th thirteenth
14th fourteenth
15th fifteenth
16th sixteenth
17th seventeenth
18th eighteenth
19th nineteenth
20th twentieth
21st twenty-first
30th thirtieth
31st thirty-first

GO BEYOND

Write your birthday and the birthdays of three people in your family. Use numbers and words.

Page 102

ADJECTIVES OF OPINION

amazing
beautiful
boring
brilliant
cool
difficult
easy
excellent
exciting
fantastic
friendly
good
happy
hard
important
interesting
lovely
popular
pretty
special
strange
useful
wonderful

GO BEYOND

Write a word from the list about:

1 your best friend
2 your home
3 your last holiday
4 your clothes today
5 you

OTHER IMPORTANT WORDS

break (v)
busy
calendar
circus
copy (v)
date
dream (n)
dream (v)
get hurt (v)
honest
I'd like …
journal
laugh (v)
lie (v)
look good (v)
machine
move (to) (v)
offer (v)
opinion
review
stay (v)
table tennis
teach (v)
the future
thousand
travel (v)
work (= function)
Would you like … ?

Page 108

RECALL

SPORTS
basketball
football
swimming
tennis

COLOURS
blue
green
red
white
yellow

CLOTHES
(football) shirt
shoes
socks
T-shirt
trainers
trousers

PARTS OF THE BODY
arm
back
ear
eye
face
foot
hand
head
leg

WORK WITH WORDS

TIP: When you learn a new word, think of other connected words.

TASK: Think of your favourite sports team and player. What colours, clothes and parts of the body do you think of? What other words do you think of?

Pages 108 and 109

PREPOSITIONS OF PLACE
above
behind
between
in
in front of
near
next to
on
opposite
under

GO BEYOND
Write six sentences about things that you can see now using different prepositions of place.

Page 112

SPORTS
baseball
cycling
golf
hockey
horse-riding
ice skating
sailing
skiing
surfing
volleyball

GO BEYOND
Match the sports to the superlatives:

1 the most exciting ....
2 the most difficult to learn ....
3 the oldest ....
4 the most dangerous ....
5 the worst ....

OTHER IMPORTANT WORDS
aim
backwards
blog post
can (n)
competition
directions
do tricks
do your best
high
hit
jump (v + n)
know your limits
net
pass (an exam)
position
racket
record (n)
spot
step
table tennis
tense (n)
toy
trainer
unhappy
What's wrong?
young

IRREGULAR VERBS

base form	past simple	past participle
agree	agreed	agreed
be	was/were	been
break	broke	broken
bring	brought	brought
buy	bought	bought
can	could	been able to
choose	chose	chosen
come	came	come
cost	cost	cost
cut	cut	cut
do	did	done
draw	drew	drawn
drink	drank	drunk
drive	drove	driven
eat	ate	eaten
fall	fell	fallen
feel	felt	felt
find	found	found
fly	flew	flown
forget	forgot	forgotten
get	got	got
give	gave	given
go	went	gone
have	had	had
hear	heard	heard
hit	hit	hit
hurt	hurt	hurt
keep	kept	kept
know	knew	known
learn	learnt/learned	learnt/learned
let	let	let

base form	past simple	past participle
lie	lay	lain
make	made	made
meet	met	met
put	put	put
read	read	read
ride	rode	ridden
run	ran	run
say	said	said
see	saw	seen
send	sent	sent
set	set	set
shake	shook	shaken
show	showed	shown
sing	sang	sung
sit	sat	sat
sleep	slept	slept
speak	spoke	spoken
spend	spent	spent
stand	stood	stood
steal	stole	stolen
swim	swam	swum
take	took	taken
teach	taught	taught
tell	told	told
think	thought	thought
understand	understood	understood
wear	wore	worn
win	won	won
withdraw	withdrew	withdrawn
write	wrote	written

STUDENT A

UNIT 2 LISTENING AND VOCABULARY

Page 24, Exercise 3

He's got a big head and he hasn't got any hair. He's got one big red eye. His nose is blue. His mouth is very small and he's only got one tooth. He's hasn't got any arms. He's got three legs and big feet.

UNIT 5 GRAMMAR

Page 57, Exercise 6

Choose one of the jobs and think of a person.

- A teacher
- An actor (male)
- A member of a pop group

UNIT 6 GRAMMAR

Page 67, Exercise 6

School trip A
Paris
Cost: €350
Days: four
Stay: in a small hotel
Activities: visit museums and famous buildings

UNIT 6 GRAMMAR

Page 69, Exercise 7

UNIT 7 GRAMMAR

Page 79, Exercise 7

Describe the picture of Bella's room to your partner. Don't look at your partner's picture. Find six differences.

UNIT 9 SPEAKING

Page 105, Exercise 5

There is cat hair everywhere at your partner's house. You don't want to eat anything there, just drink something.

ALL STUDENTS

UNIT 3 LISTENING AND VOCABULARY

Page 36, Exercise 5b

UNIT 10 IN THE PICTURE

Page 108, Exercise 4b

Were Alan and Kayla right? Were you right?

STUDENT B

UNIT 2 LISTENING AND VOCABULARY

Page 24, Exercise 3

She's got a small head and red hair. Her eyes are pink and her face is green. She hasn't got a nose. She's got big ears and a big mouth. Her teeth are yellow. She's got one arm. She's got two legs and four feet.

UNIT 5 GRAMMAR

Page 57, Exercise 6

Choose one of the jobs and think of a person.

- A famous football player
- An actor (female)
- A famous cook or a cook at your school

UNIT 6 GRAMMAR

Page 67, Exercise 6

School trip B
Film studio
Cost: €190
Days: five
Stay: in tents
Activities: learn about films, make a short film

UNIT 6 GRAMMAR

Page 69, Exercise 7

UNIT 7 GRAMMAR

Page 79, Exercise 7

Describe the picture of Bella's room to your partner. Don't look at your partner's picture. Find six differences.

UNIT 9 SPEAKING

Page 105, Exercise 5

You don't like sandwiches or anything with meat.

ALL STUDENTS

UNIT 10 IN THE PICTURE

Page 109, Exercise 8b

Were you right?

STEP-BY-STEP PROJECTS

Download more information from www.macmillanbeyond.com.

MAKE A COLLAGE

- Make a list of parts of the body – *hand, eyes, legs* … .
- Find photos of body parts in old magazines and newspapers.
- Cut out your photos and make the collage.

Units 1 & 2

FORM A BAND

- Choose a type of band – *pop, hip hop, rock* … .
- Choose instruments to play – *drums, guitar, keyboard* … .
- Give your band a name and write profiles for the band members.

Units 3 & 4

DESIGN A DREAM HOME

- Choose a famous person to design the home for – *sports personality, film star, singer* … .
- List special things to include in the home – *gym, cinema, studio* … .
- Choose a location and design the home.

Units 5 & 6

PRESENT THE WEATHER

- Choose a location – *a country, a city, your local area* … .
- Prepare the weather forecast. Include a report and sound effects.
- Present your weather report.

Units 7 & 8

MAKE A CALENDAR

- Choose the time period for the calendar – *this week, month, school holidays* … .
- Make a list of important dates – *birthdays, holidays, anniversaries* … .
- Make your calendar with the information and pictures.

Units 9 & 10

Macmillan Education
4 Crinan Street
London N1 9XW
A division of Springer Nature Limited
Companies and representatives throughout the world
ISBN 978-0-230-46101-7

First published 2015

Designed by emc design ltd

Illustrated by Seb Camagajevac (Beehive Illustration) p 78; Peter Cornwell pp 34, 35 (l), 36, 141 (Unit 6 Grammar), 142 (Unit 6 Grammar); Tom Croft pp 29, 48; Venitia Dean (Advocate-Art) p97; Sally Elford pp 10 (music notes), 20 (people), 25, 32 (clock, coins, computer), 42 (cello, tv, books, CDs, shopping), 54 (menu, till, clock), 64 (onion, bed, bowl), 86 (banner artwork), 98 (invitation), 108 (cricket bat, football, table tennis paddle, skates, wheelchair, tennis ball); Kev Hopgood pp 23, 35 (r), 38, 44, 47, 67, 81, 84, 113, 141 (Unit 3 Listening and Vocabulary); Bob Lea pp 54-55; Caron Painter (Sylvie Poggio Artists) pp 16, 19 (bottom), 21, 40, 85, 88, 95, 100, 101, 117, 141 (Unit 7 Grammar), 142 (Unit 7 Grammar); Zara Picken p 24; Jamie Pogue (Bright Agency) pp 6, 7, 8, 9; David Shephard (Bright Agency) pp 12, 99 (boy ill in bed), 114, Tony Wilkins pp 58, 86-87 (map) Tony Forbes (Sylvie Poggio Artists) pp 15.

Cover design by emc design ltd
Cover photographs by **Alamy**/Brentonwest (full page), Alamy/Olga Miltsova
Picture research by Emily Taylor

The authors would like to thank all the team at Macmillan in the UK, Mexico, Poland, Spain and the rest of the world for everything they've done to make Beyond possible. Special thanks to our commissioning editor, managing editor and our publisher for their endless hard work and encouragement. We'd like to thank Studio 8 for their creative work on the drama group videos and EMC for coming up with the Beyond design concept. We'd also like to thank all the teachers and other individuals who have contributed to the course whose names appear on this page. A special thank you to Jade Todd and Jim Connolly for providing us with the wonderful free-time activity photos in Unit 4. Finally, we'd like to thank our friends and families for all their support.

The authors and publishers would like to express thanks to all those who contributed to the development and formation of Beyond. In particular, we would like to thank the following teachers, contacts and reviewers: Cristina Moisén Antón, Argelia Solis Arriaga, Krzysztof Bartold, Paweł Bienert, Agnieszka Bojanowska, Samuel Gómez Borobia, Ma. Eugenia Fernández Castro, Jolanta Chojnacka, Elsa Georgina Cruz, Dominika Dąbrowska, Barbara Dawidowska, Galina Dragunova, Monika Drygiel-Kobylińska, Mauricio Duran, Natalia Evdokimenko, Maria Teresa Velázquez Evers, Marciana Loma-Osorio Fontecha, Monika Fromiczew-Drożdzińska, Patricia García, Axel Morales García, Miguel Angel Rodriguez García, Aleksandra Gilewska, Joanna Góra, Ewa Górka, Daphne Green, Agata Helwich, Bethsabe Ruiz Herrera, Robert Jadachowski, Patricia Guzmán Luis Juan, Anna Kacpura, Ruth Kanter, Regina Kaźmierczuk, Katarzyna Konisiewicz, Maria Koprowska, Bogusława Krajewska, Aldona Krasoń, Joanna Worobiec Kugaj, Joanna Kuligowska, Tadeusz Kur, Maria Kwiatkowska, Josefina Maitret, Javier Majul, Claire Manners, Laura Elena Medina, Carmen García Méndez, Iwona Mikucka, Talhia Miranda, Claudia Rangel Miranda, Armando Nieto, Joanna Nowak, Anna Nowakowska, Ewa Nowicka, Anastasia Parshikova, Paloma Carrasco Peñalba, Ma. Del Carmen Fernández Pérez, Joanna Płatos, Louise Emma Potter, Maria Teresa Portillo, Juan José Gómez Ramírez, Aida Rivera, Gabriela Rubio, Gabriela Bourge Ruiz, Irina Sakharova, Małgorzata Sałaj, Patricia Avila Sánchez, Jessica Galvan Sanchez, Miguel Angel Santiago, Karol Sęk, Barbara Sibilska, Tatiana Sinyavina, Agnieszka Śliwowska, Vlada Songailene, Ángela Siles Suárez, Beata Świątkowska, Ewelina Szmyd-Patuła, Agnieszka Szymaniak, Juliana Maria Franco Tavares, José Luis Vázquez, Irma Velazquez, Małgorzata Walczak, Dariusz Winiarek, Justyna Zdunek, Zofia Żdżarska, Dominika Zięba, Marzena Zieleniewska, Anna Zielińska-Miszczuk, Robert Zielonka.

The authors and publishers would also like to thank the following schools who allowed class observations – MEXICO: Centro de Formación Escolar Banting, Centro Escolar Las Águilas, Colegio América, Colegio Axayacatl, Colegio Donato Bramante, Colegio Edgar Morin, Colegio Francés Nueva Santa María, Colegio Gesi Secundaria, Colegio José Martí S. C., Colegio San Agustin, Colegio Sir Winston Leonard Spencer Churchill De México, Colegios La Salle Boulevares, Cristian Fernández de Merino, Erasmo De Rótterdam, Escuela De Ruán, Grupo Colegio Rosario Castellanos, Instituto Atenea, Instituto Crisol, Instituto Cultural Americano Mexicano, Instituto Manuel Acosta, Instituto Oriente Arboledas, Instituto Zaragoza, Liceo Americano Francés, Liceo Ibero Mexicano, Liceo Mexicano Japonés, Secundaria Simón Bolívar. SPAIN: IES Anselmo Lorenzo, IES Camilo José Cela, IES Complutense, IES Joaquín Turina, IES Laguna de Joatzell, IES Luis García Berlanga, IES Manuel de Falla, IES Máximo Trueba. POLAND: Gimnazjum nr 30, Gimnazjum nr 104 Warszawa Wawer, Gimnazjum nv120, Gimnazjum nr 141, Gimnazjum nr 145, Gimnazjum, ul. SZKOLNA 4, Publiczne Gimnazjum w Wiązownie, ZSP w Jazgarzewie. TURKEY: Ahmet Şimşek Koleji, Anabilim Koleji, Büyük Çamlıca Koleji, Doğa Koleji, Kirimli Fazilet Olcay Anatolian High School, Modafen Koleji, Sakıp Sabancı Anadolu Lisesi.

The authors and publishers would like to thank the following for permission to reproduce their photographs:

Alamy p11(x) "Used with permission from Microsoft.", Alamy/42pix Premier p90(c), Alamy/AF archive p24(5), Alamy/Aflo Co. Ltd p110(br), Alamy/Age fotostock p70(tl), Alamy/All Star Photographs p24(3), Alamy/Angela Hampton Picture Library p103, Alamy/Arco Images pp32(c), 33(h), Alamy/Aurora Photosp65(br), Alamy/Beyond Fotomedia pp108(b), 141(br), Alamy/Big Cheese Photo LLC p25, Alamy/Richard G. Bingham II p37(tl), Alamy/Blickwinkel p87(cr), Alamy/Bubbles Photolibrary p118, Alamy/Thomas Cockrem p92(tmr), Alamy/Bea Cooper p64(cr), Alamy/Leila Cutler pp21(1), 22(felix), Alamy/Darren Green Photography p86(tr), Alamy/EPA/Sergei Chirikov p87(tr), Alamy/Betty Finney p65(tr, cm), Alamy/Viktor Fischer p13(6), Alamy/Paul Fleet p81, Alamy/Foodfolio p69, Alamy/Eric Fowke p89(bm), Alamy/Forget Patrick/Sagaphoto.com p37(inset), Alamy/Clare Gainey p82(tr), Alamy/Bernardo Galmarini p86(cr), Alamy/Glow Images Asia p92(tml), Alamy/Bill Gozansky p65(cl), Alamy/David Hancock pp109(b), 142(br), Alamy/Tim Hill p33(e), Alamy/Andrew Holt p62, Alamy/Doug Houghton p72(bl), Alamy/Huntstock Inc p28(2), Alamy/Imagebroker pp90(b), 32(a), Alamy/Image Source pp52, 64(cm), 82(cm), Alamy/Juniors Bildarchiv GmbH p33(j), Alamy/Kevers p12(br), Alamy/Andrey Kuzmin p11(l), Alamy/LOOK Die Bildagentur der Fotografen p90(a), Alamy/Dennis MacDonald pp108(a), Alamy/Oleksiy Maksymenko p143(tr), 141(bmrr), Alamy/Barry Mason p13(1), Alamy/Keith Morris p21(5), Alamy/Peter Adams Photography Ltd p12(tr), Alamy/Picture Partners p26, Alamy/Thibaut Petit-Bara p73(tr), Alamy/Purestock p114(tl), Alamy/Radius Images pp14(cr), 106(Dario), Alamy/Andres Rodriguez p11(n), Alamy/Ed Rooney p82(tl), Alamy/RT Images pp12(cm), 37(tr), Alamy/Rubberball p11(z), Alamy/Kumar Sriskandan p32(b), Alamy/Mick Sinclair p82(cr), Alamy/Susie Slatter p33(i), Alamy/StockbrokerXtra p91(br), Alamy/Peter Titmuss p86(br), p87(br), Alamy/Top-Pet-Pics p34, Alamy/Vibe Images pp109(c), 141(bmr), Alamy/Jan Wlodarczyk p66(tml), Alamy/YAY Media AS p11(v);
BananaStock pp10(r), 11(i), 19, 21(7), 70(tml);
Brand X Pictures pp64(bm), 54(8);
Comstock Images p68(j);
Corbis pp11(e), Corbis p54(1,2,4), Corbis/Atlantide Phototravel p66(tr), Corbis/Blend p11(u), Corbis/EPA p110(cr), Corbis/Floresco Productions pp21(6), 22(Asha), Corbis/Ned Frisk p11g, Corbis/James Leynse p82(br), Cobis/Tom Martin/JAI p64(tr), Corbis/Ocean pp45(tr), 66(tl), Corbis/Sebastian Pfuetze p21(9), Corbis/Martin Siepmann/Westend61 p33(d), Corbis/Grady Reese p70(tr), Corbis/Gregor Schuster p11(w), Corbis/Michael Zegers p66(tmr);
Digital Vision p68(k);
Getty Images pp10(b,f), 68(a,b,h,l), Getty Images/Don Bayley p11(y), Getty Images/Peter Cade p79, Getty Images/Elisa Cicinelli p53(cl), Getty Images/Stewart Cohen p21(3), Getty Images/Compassionate Eye Foundation/Robert Daly/OJO Images p60, Getty Images/Cultura p21(2), Getty Images/Cultura/Luc Beziat p22(Leon), Getty Images/Stuart Dee p24(1), Getty Images/Flickr Open p114(tr), Getty Images/Flickr RF pp56(cl), Getty Images/Fuse p143(bl), Getty Images/Vanessa Gavalya p28(1), Getty Images/John Giustina p112, Getty Images/Gorilla RM/Petri Artturi Asikainen, p91(tl), Getty Images/Hiroshi Higuchi p96, Getty Images/Hill Street Studios p30, Getty Images/Lonely Planet p90(d), Getty Images/Neva MoAnik p28(3), Getty Images/National Geographic Creative p94, Getty Images/Jose Luis Pelaez p114(tm), Getty Images/PureStock p104, Getty Images/Gregory Shamus/NBAE p111 - Used with Permission, Getty Images/Tetra images p45(tl), Getty Images/Kutay Tanir p143(br), Getty Images/Kerstin Waurick p53(cl), Getty Images/Westend61 p89(tl), Getty Images/Ziva_K p53(cm);
ImageSource pp10(k), 13(2), 70(tmr), 92(tr), 109(a), 142(bl);
iStock pp13(tl),
Macmillan Publishing Ltd pp10(a), 11(d), 23, 54(6), 68(i,g), 143(tl);
PA Images/AP p110(cl);
PhotoAlto p21(4);
Photodisc pp64(cl, cr), PhotoDisc/Getty Imagesp68(c,d);
Photoshot/Andia p24(2);
Plain Picture p11(h), Plain Picture/Siegfried Kuttig p116, Plain Picture/PhotoAlto p18(cr), Plain Picture/Romulic-Stojcic p56(tr);
Rex Features/Startraks Photo p24(4);
Stockbyte/PunchStock p67;
Stock Illustrations Ltd p143(tl);
SuperStock pp33(g,f), 54(7), SuperStock/Bill Gozansky p65(cm);
ThinkStock pp10(q), 11(c,j,o,p,s,t), 54(3,5), 68(e,f), 106(Andrei), 118, ThinkStock/Getty Images/Fuse p46(3), ThinkStock/Getty Images/iStockphoto pp13(3,4,5), 14(sunglasses), 18(cl, cm), 44(boy, inset), 46(1,4,5), 64(bl), ThinkStock/Getty Images/Hemera p46(2), ThinkStock/iStock pp11(m), 50, 143(cr), ThinkStock/Jupiterimages/Brand X Pictures p14(cl), ThinkStock/Moodboard p14(cm).

Commissioned photography by Jim Connolly and Jade Todd pp42–43; Studio 8 Limited pp17, 27, 39, 49, 61, 71, 76, 77, 80, 83, 93, 99, 105 and 115

Printed in Dimograf, Poland.
2018
14